D1236709

"Muñecas"

A Memoir

By: Leticia Cervantes-Lopez

ISBN: 9798398343939

Printed in the United States of America

Book Layout and Artwork designed by:

Garrett and Amber Mcgurer

Acknowledgment

First of all, I thank God and the Blessed Mother for their blessings.
I dedicate this book to the memory of both my son
Xavier Cervantes-Lopez and my husband Jose Maria Lopez Becerra
To my sons, Eduardo, Ricardo, and Alexandro, whose love completes my life.
And to their wives, Paola, Jackie, and Tetiana.
Much Love to my little blessings: Viviana, Miranda, Lucia, and Matilda
Special thanks: to my family, my parents:
Jose and Benita Cervantes, and my sisters Sylvia, Connie, Carmen, and
Lucy Cervantes, for all their love and support in carrying me through this journey
In gratitude to the entire *Lopez Becerra Family*, to Domitila Becerra
And the village of La Laja for their unselfish love and support.
For sharing their life stories and love and support for me and Chema in our journey
Much love and gratitude to Diana Estrada and Norma Acosta-Sanchez.
Thank you, Dr. Nina Newell, for your guidance
Thank you, Chelsy Alcazar, for the Authors photo, and editing process
Much love to my family of friends at WUHSD and WUHSD Categorical Program
For all their love, understanding, and for totally supporting my dreams

I am truly BLESSED
To little Eddie and future generations.

Table of Contents

This Memoir pertains to my personal life and experiences during the first five years of marriage, and to the loss of my young son. It is written with much love and pain from my perspective. Some names and situations are changed to respect and protect some real characters in the story.

LAMENTS OF EVE

Sharp stabbing in my waist, back, and thighs

The fiery knife of life inside me.

Cracking bones like burning coals. Tearing the flesh, it

passes

Lenient and strong like a forceful soldier of war

sharp claws tearing my flesh so deep

Sweating and pushing with all my might

to give a new life a chance

Departing with something that grew inside me

Finally, the last push! The Last effort!

the holy cry of life begins.

The pain and grief are forgotten

A new life begins, a new little love!

Laments of Eve Forgotten

January 1, 1982

CHAPTER 1
IN THE DELIVERY ROOM

The bright lights in the delivery room ceiling hover over me like the hot sun. The heat of the two large lamps is directly above me, making me feel more tense and uncomfortable in my position. My legs are mounted and spread, ready to deliver my baby. Although I'm very happy that this day is finally here, I hope this will be over soon. After eighteen hours of hard child labor, my baby is not as anxious as me to finally get here. Although very exhausted, I happily wait for my second baby to arrive. I'm trying to gather all that I have left in me to continue labor. The miracle of life is near! What a blessing it is to have a baby growing inside my body. I can't wait to finally hold and see him/her in my arms."

A nurse now encourages me to take some deep breaths and to try to relax before pushing again. Jose is standing beside me, holding my hand and encouraging me to continue the good work. Having my husband here really helps me to relax and continue. The doctor now asks me to give it my all, that the baby's head is crowning. I feel excited now, and a new surge of energy suddenly comes over me. I feel a strong urge to push. In a combination of sweat and tears, I gather all the strength left in me to give the final push. Squeezing Jose's hand, I shut my eyes and pushed as hard as I could. Suddenly I can feel a warm gush exiting my body. I now know the baby has arrived!

"The baby is here!" Jose tells me with tears in his eyes as he strokes my wet hair back out of my wet face. "You did great," he tells me as he warmly kisses my forehead. "It's another boy!" He repeats with joy. I can't help but also cry joyful tears. "Life is a true miracle and a gift of God!" "*Gracias Señor Jesús.*" Jose softly caresses and kisses my hand, and thanks me for giving him another beautiful son. By now I'm overwhelmed with happiness to finally have another child. "Our little family is now complete," I tell Jose. I have experienced this immense ecstasy with my first son before; it's a sense of heavenly joy and indescribable delight to give birth to another human being. "God has trusted us in giving us another angel to take care of," I tell Jose, and he agrees.

But within seconds, our joy and happiness are short-lived when we quickly come to realize that there is an unusual silence in the delivery room. Something is wrong! The usual immediate sound of a crying baby is missing. "My baby is not crying!" I scream with all my might. "Why isn't my baby crying?" I then see Jose's face turn a different color as he moves forward to take a closer look at the baby. I could tell by the worried look he had on his face when he realized the baby's umbilical cord wrapped around his little neck. Slowly Jose walks back to my bed and, in trying not to scare me, or knowing what to say, stands quietly by me. Jose holds my hand and says, "Everything will be alright."

Soon two nurses and the doctor carefully work to unwrap the cord. I can see them taking the baby to a small examining table away from my sight. The bright lights above the table are immediately lit, and the three make a small circle around the baby. They then begin to whisper a sort of secret among themselves. By now I frantically try to lift myself by holding on to the bed rails. I lift myself from the bed as long as I can, but I'm unable to stay sitting. I am too weak. So I then lay back in bed and demanded to know what was going on. Just then, Jose turns to me and begs me to "calm down." "That the doctor is working on our son and to be patient, that the doctor knows what he's doing." I then decided to just lay down and quietly pray.

For me, the short time not hearing the baby cry feels like an eternity. It has only been a few seconds, but these seconds feel like minutes and even hours. I begged Jose to describe to me what he could see. And by now, Jose's face seems somewhat nervous to say anything to me. Suddenly he quickly calls out to the doctor demanding answers.

Finally, a nurse quickly comes to us to explain: "The baby was born with the umbilical cord wrapped twice around his neck; this is the reason he's not crying yet. The doctor is working on the baby as fast and as safely as he could." She assures us that "these are the usual steps and procedures taken with babies born in this condition." "The baby will cry in seconds, I promise." She says, "Everything will be alright, you'll see. In less than a minute, you will hear your son cry." Again, waiting a few seconds feels like long minutes.

At last, we hear a low and soft whimper, a sort of faint cry finally coming from the baby. "It sounds like the cry of a little lamb or kitten but not at all like a baby," I say to Jose. "Is he crying? Is he alright?" Jose tells me with great relief. "Yes, the baby is crying!" "I hear his crying too," "But Jose, it sounds weak and very unusual; it's not a normal cry for a newborn baby."

"Don't exaggerate *mujer,*" Jose somewhat nervously turns to me and says: "Calm down, it's our son crying. He is just a little tired because of all the hard labor and trauma he has gone through." "He is all right; I'm sure of that. I think that you're just too tired and confused right now. You had a long labor, and right now, your thinking is confused, that's all."

I listen to Jose's words, but my heart tells me otherwise, and I am unsure why. My mother's instinct tells me something is wrong with my baby's weak cry. "It's not a strong cry," I insist. Jose once again held my hand to remind me, "You heard what the nurse said; the umbilical cord was tied tightly around his little neck. He will be fine". Jose takes my hand up to his heart to comfort me and convinces me that everything will be alright.

I must confess that I am grateful for my son finally crying, even if it's an unusual cry. Thinking this, a sigh of relief suddenly comes over me. I think to myself that he could have died in the birth canal. I take a deep breath and listen to Jose's advice. I ask the nurse if I can hold my baby. The nurse nods in agreement and prepares the baby to finally bring him to my arms.

Having my new son in my arms for the first time was a beautiful feeling. The first thing I notice about him is the ashy, grayish color on his little face. His little lips are blue and not the usual pink color a baby should have. Holding my son, I can feel his very frail little body wrapped in a soft blanket. "Why is my baby so small and blue?" I quickly called out to the doctor! "Please tell me, is there anything else wrong with him?" The doctor quickly comes to me and explains. "The baby has gone through a lot of trauma and stress coming down the birth canal; he was struggling for some time there. Unfortunately, having the umbilical cord wrapped around his neck twice didn't help his breathing situation. The cord is what kept him in the birth canal longer than usual. That is why his appearance is ashy and blue. But he should be fine in a few days."

Jose accepts the doctor's explanation, but I have some doubts and reservations. I'm not sure why my heart tells me something else is going on. Somehow deep inside me, I feel that there is more to the doctor's story, and I don't know what that is. I try to convince myself that I'm overthinking like Jose says. I tell myself that all my doubts are because I'm tired and overthinking. Now I have to convince myself that my baby is going to be fine.

The nurses advised Jose to leave the room so they could finish with me taking care of the final stages of the delivery. Jose told me that he would be downstairs waiting for us to be in our room. Now my son is kindly taken from me by the nurse, but this time he is only a few steps away from me, where I could see the nurse cleaning him and taking his footprint. The doctor prepares me for some stitches, and with that done, he gets me set to go to my room with my baby. Holding my son in my arms, all my physical pain is forgotten.

Chapter 2
Leaving the Delivery Room

January 1, 1982 Mid-afternoon

After all the prepping in the delivery room, the baby and I are finally taken to our hospital room. I hold my son close to me as we are wheeled down through the bright long hallways. Entering the room, I can feel the air conditioning is on very high, and I immediately ask the nurse for a warm blanket. Once finally placed in my bed with warm blankets, I hold my son in my arms, close to my heart. The baby's eyes are wide open by now but very swollen. The nurse put a sort of gel on them; she says to help his eyes adjust to the light in the room.

I now look around the room, and right in front of me, I see a large window with the shades wide open, displaying a beautiful bright sunny day outside. "Happy

New Year," the nurse tells me. "It's 1982," she says with a smile. "Happy New Year," I answered her not so enthusiastically. The sun is bright, and I can see birds flying from tree to tree directly outside the window. "Thank you, God, for your blessings" "Thank you, Blessed Mother for letting me start a new year with a brand new baby" I feel so blessed to be with my baby. "Blessed Mother, please let my son be alright"

I turn to the side of the room and am pleasantly surprised to see a beautiful bouquet of white roses in a large glass vase sitting at a night table beside my bed. "They are from your husband," the nurse says as she fixes the blankets around me. "Aren't they beautiful? He said he would return to see you in a few minutes''. 'Thank you for telling me," I told her. And now, the nurse points to the phone and tells me, "Please call if you need anything. I will be in the station right outside this door; please rest. You need to be rested because soon your baby will want to eat, and you will be breastfeeding him." The nurse kindly touches my hand, fixes my pillows, then leaves the room.

I now take another deep breath and look at my little son who by now is looking straight at me. "I was told you barely weigh five pounds, little one": "I'm sorry you've been through so much to get here, being so little and all. It's been two days of struggle for you my baby, but you made it here with me; you're here! Now we can rest and recover together from all this my son. I love you," I tell him as I kiss his little soft forehead. "You are a blessing and a real miracle for me today, my little one." "You are my Angel." The baby is still staring at me like telling me something. "Sleep little one," I tell him softly, ''*Duermete mi niño.*"

Within minutes, Jose walks into the room holding a beautiful stuffed fluffy white bunny in his hands. "This is for the baby," he says smiling. He places the bunny on the side of the bed where the baby is and bends over to kiss both of us. "Thank you for my roses," I told him very lovingly. "You're very welcome," he tells me in the same loving tone. "I know they're your favorite." I thank him again with a kiss and let him know how much I love him. Looking at his tired face, I can tell that he too is very exhausted. I try to convince him to go home and get some rest. "It's been two long days of not sleeping for you too." I say to him, "You need to go home and sleep." "I will go soon," he says, almost yawning. "But first I want to hold my son for a bit." Jose gently takes the baby from my arms and into his and caresses him in a very loving way. He looks towards me and says, "He looks like you." I smile, but he seems to notice the concern on my face for the baby. He just knows me very well. He reminds me of what the doctor says about the baby's color becoming normal in one or two days. I see Jose holding our son so close to him and see the love radiating between father and son, and right there, and then a thought comes over me. "Jose, let's name our baby *Xavier. It means "New and Bright" in Arabic. And "he who brings light* in French." Jose thinks about it for a second and says, without any doubt in his mind. "His name is Xavier, then!" Looking at the baby, Jose says, it's a perfect name for you, my son. "I believe Xavier is here to give us light," I tell Jose. "My son has a name now, and it's a perfect name, Xavier!"

The thought that something is wrong with my baby still bothers me. I know Jose can tell this when he sees my face and says. "It's only natural that you worry. You are a very caring mother. But it's all going to be alright, you'll see. Let's just be glad that the baby is alive and here in our arms right now. Because a few hours ago in the delivery room, we didn't think he would make it. Think about that."

"You're right," I say to Jose. "I'm so glad he's alive." I thank God he's here with us, a good rest will bring me peace of mind." "That's my girl," he tells me as he hands and places the baby back in my arms. "I will be back in a few hours. I'm going home to rest'', he says as he kisses me. "Have a good rest, I tell him." "You too," he answers as he kisses my forehead once more, and leaves the room. Now the baby and I lay warmly in our bed together, sharing our first wonderful sleep as mother and child. "Happy New Year, Happy 1982," I say to myself as I hold my son close to my heart and slowly fall asleep.

Chapter 3
Xavier Goes Home and Meets the Family

January 3, 1982

One afternoon, two days after giving birth, my son and I were released and sent home from the hospital. Although little Xavier's color hasn't changed, I'm so happy to finally be going home to my son Eddie, whom I know is happily waiting for our arrival. Eddie is anxious to meet his little brother for the first time. Our drive home is peaceful and exciting. I am very anxious to hold Eddie in my arms once again. And he is anxious to finally meet his little brother.

Upon arrival in the driveway, I can see Eddie's little eager face filled with anticipation to see Mama and Papa again. My mother is holding him onto him, sitting on the porch waiting for us to drive into the driveway and finally stop the car. When we turn off the car, my mother releases him, and Eddie runs towards the driveway and directly to me. My heart jumps with joy seeing him so excited. "Mama, mama," he says as we embrace. Jose says, "What about me, buddy?" I want a hug too." Eddie runs to Jose, and Jose raises him up in the air as Eddie likes it. "I'm an airplane. I can fly!" Eddie says in delight as Jose spins him around. With this, I think and feel back to my usual self again.

"I want to see my brother now," Eddie says as Jose puts him back on the ground. Eddie walks over to meet baby Xavier. Eddie holds the baby close to him. I can tell he loved his brother from the very beginning. He is so loving and kind to him and caresses him. With wide eyes and a big smile, Eddie looks at the baby and kisses him. "He's my new little brother?" he asks me. "Yes, *mijo,* this is Xavier, your little brother," I tell him. Looking down at Xavier with a smile, he enthusiastically says: "I will share all my toys with him. When can I play with him?" He eagerly asks, "Not now, Papa says, but soon you can play with him when he gets a little older. For now, let's go inside the house where Mama can rest, and you can hold your new little brother"

We all go inside the house, ready to start our new life as a family. My mother and I finally embrace, and she sits on the sofa holding the baby. By the look on her face, I can tell she too also notices the baby's blue-grayish color and frail state. "What is wrong with the baby?" she asks me with concern. Jose quickly jumps in and slowly explains the situation with the bay to her. I now hold and play with Eddie and it gives me a good feeling of being back home. "It will soon be all right with the baby in a few days," Jose assures my mother. I can tell my mother is somehow not convinced by that explanation.

As she holds Xavier, my mother says: "This is so unusual. I've never seen this in the family." "God willing, the baby's color will be normal soon, you'll see. My mother tries to reassure me with words. Her eyes barely meet mine, and I can tell she is hiding her worry. Neither of us has a smile on our faces.

The day ends with my mother leaving us with a full dinner on the stove. "Eddie had his dinner about an hour ago." I thank my mother as she gets ready to leave. " I'll be back in the morning," she tells me as she puts her sweater on. "Gracias, mama, for everything," I tell her as she gets her keys from her purse and leaves.

Trying hard to think good and better thoughts, I say: "Our new life begins now. "Life is good," I say to Jose as I'm putting the baby in his baby bassinet. Jose nods his head in agreement and puts Eddie down, who by now is fast asleep. With both boys asleep, Jose and I sit on the ha living room sofa holding each in total silence. At this time, there are no words needed. We both know that all we have to live by is the "now," and take each day at a time. We realize that the future of our little family is uncertain.

Jose insists that I should eat something. "You haven't eaten much all day or even all week," he tells me. We both decide to get up from the sofa and make our way to the kitchen table and try to eat something. Jose serves me a small plate and sits with me while sipping his coffee and eating a *pan dulce*. In between bites, our eyes meet, but again say nothing. Our eyes are blank, like getting ready for a whole new beginning. A beginning complete with a brand new year, 1982. A year that we both hope and pray will be as good as before. A year we hope will be full of blessings.

After a while at the kitchen table, we decided to get up and get ready for bed. We both knew that the baby's next feeding would be soon. Once in our bed together, we hold on to one another; it's all we can do for each other's comfort. In the silence of the night, we can feel our souls speaking softly to each other, consoling our thoughts all at once. My husband is me, and I am my husband.

Xavier comes home from the hospital and meets Eddie

January 1982

Chapter 4
The Family Meets Baby Xavier
January 4, 1982

Today, our families and close friends are coming to our house to meet Xavier for the first time finally. Everyone anxiously calls Jose, asking him for the arrival time at our house. By midday, the backyard is decorated with blue and white balloons and a beautiful homemade welcome home sign that says: WELCOME HOME, BABY Xavier." Soon everyone arrives at our house with food, drinks, and a cake to welcome the sweet baby.

We, the happy parents, enter the backyard through the back door where the family awaits. Jose holds Eddie in his arms as I walk in with Xavier in mine. Soon after greetings with everyone, Grandmother takes the baby from me, ready to show him off to the aunts and uncles. I can tell that the family notices Xavier's frail little face and his pale color, but no one asks Jose or me anything about it. They are being cautious and polite so as not to worry us. I know my mother has explained the situation to most of them, and they are all being nice and not asking anything about the baby's appearance.

With Eddie in my arms, I begin to enjoy everyone's company. The food is delicious, and the family has light, happy conversations about Eddie and the other children in the family. How they have been playing and doing amazing things the last few days. Everyone is eating and enjoying the baby and each other's company. Xavier is being carefully and lovingly passed amongst family. I feel so happy to see and feel all the love around us. As the day of celebration continues, I stay close to Eddie to let him know that he is not being replaced by his brother and tell him that they will soon be playing together. He likes this; he shows me with his smile.

The end of the day comes quickly, and family and friends begin to leave. Some family members help Jose clean the backyard, and I go inside to feed Xavier and for him to get a much-needed rest. So far today, Xavier has been a good baby by not crying or fussing much. This surprises me. But soon, that is cut short, and Xavier begins to cry like he is not feeling well. My heart tells me now he has some sort of discomfort. Maybe due to being held by mostly everyone for most of the day. I then realize that it has been a long and unusual day for him or any newborn.

At the end of the day, and for the first time in a long time, I'm feeling complete as a mother and a wife. I'm home, and I feel blessed to be enjoying my sons, husband, and my whole family all together. The first day home has been a success. The family came and left the yard and the kitchen spotless, and there was leftover food in the refrigerator for us to eat later. Once everyone is gone, Jose decides to take Eddie for his bath so that I can tend to Xavier, who is, by now, very fussy. While family and friends were here for a few hours, I almost forgot Xavier's situation. But hearing Xavier's cry and his fussiness tells me that having two babies to tend to will be very different.

CHAPTER 5
TRYING TO HAVE NORMALITY

JANUARY 5, 1982

The past four days at home go by, and not much to my surprise, Xavier requires much more help and attention than I anticipated. I have discovered that he has far more unique needs than we were told. He must be fed very slowly and in a specific position to prevent his frail little body from choking. He is not doing well with breast milk, so now he is being fed a special protein formula for his small size. And because of his trouble breathing, he has trouble sleeping for more than thirty minutes at a time. This adds more to his fuzziness and his discomfort. All this is scaring me. I called the doctor for the third time today, and the nurse told me that his situation should only last one or two more days now.

Our day and night schedules are unpredictable, especially for me. By now, I sleep very little at night and in the daytime even less. I try to divide my time between Xavier's and Eddie's needs. "Why does my baby brother cry, mama?" Eddie asks me with curiosity. I tell him, "The baby is having a hard time for now and that he will be alright soon." "Why can't I hold him yet?" he asks. "You will soon," I tell him. I can tell Eddie feels something is happening with his little brother. I think his concern in his questions and little heart as he hugs me, trying to make me feel better.

Doing the house chores is challenging, but sometimes my sisters and sister-in-law come to help as much as they can. I do what I can when the boys are asleep, which is not much time for Xavier. Jose helps me with Xavier's feedings at night, and he sometimes hardly sleeps. It's been four days since arriving at the hospital, and things are not improving.

Aside from everything that's happening with our sleep schedules, Jose continues with his usual morning routine, getting up at almost dawn, having his coffee, and heading out to work. Our lives have shifted 180 degrees. Minutes feel like hours, and days feel like weeks. By now I begin to worry even more because Xavier is now in so much more discomfort. His color remains cyanotic blue, and he is constantly crying and gets very restless. With all that, he gets very little rest.

By now I can feel Xavier's crying in my gut. I try to remind myself that this is normal, as the doctor says. I tell myself, "I'm only 23 years old and know nothing about medicine. I have no experience, and I must be patient and rely on the doctor's expertise." I need to accept what he says, to survive this. I have no choice, at least for these few days. Taking or even understanding what is happening with my son has become challenging. It's all some sort of a strange, mysterious puzzle that has come to turn our lives completely upside down. I feel it's all getting out of control.

CHAPTER 6
NO CHANGE IN XAVIER
JANUARY 7, 1982

It's day six, and again, I see no change in Xavier's condition. I'm sitting in the kitchen trying to have a normal morning with Eddie, and feeding him breakfast has become a real challenge. Xavier's baby carrier is sitting on the kitchen table, where he is primarily fussy and uncomfortable. Again Eddie is constantly asking more questions about his brother. "Why does he always throw up his milk?" Again, Eddie's questions tear at my soul, and I'm not sure what to say or what to answer him. I am going somewhat crazy trying to handle this whole situation without scaring Eddie even more.

By now, tears of frustration have begun to run down my face, and I try to hide them from Eddie, but I can't fool him. Soon he too, stops eating his breakfast and begins to make a face like wanting to cry. " Mama, don't cry anymore," He says to me. "I'm ok *mijo*" I tell him as I quickly wipe the tears off my face and pick him up from his high chair. "Don't worry, baby, your brother and I are just really tired. That's why we cry. We will be ok once we take a nap."

Now that Xavier has quieted down, I take Eddie to the living room. I assure him that everything is going to be all better soon. I kiss his cheek, and he kisses me back. I sit with him on the sofa with his stuffed animals and turn on the TV to watch his favorite morning cartoons. "I like it when you sit with me to watch TV Mama," he says with a smile. But sitting with him only lasted a few short minutes. Xavier soon begins to cry, and I have to tend to him. I don't like Eddie seeing Xavier or me in this state, so now that Eddie's busy watching TV, I decided to call my mother and ask her if she or my sister can take Eddie for a few days. I explain that I cannot care for him now without worrying about him. "You sound terrible," my mother says. " Mama, you know that Eddie is a compassionate child. And now I feel that the situation here at home is getting to him and is getting out of control for me. "Please help me," I said, sobbing. My mother and sister both understood and got to my house in minutes without further explanation or delay.

CHAPTER 7
THE CRISIS
JANUARY 8, 1982

It's the beginning of the eighth day, and Javieir's little face is still grayish blue. He had a terrible night, and so did Jose and I. There is no real change in his frail little body. By now, his cry seems to be with more significant discomfort. I'm almost going out of my mind with concern. I quickly decided to call the doctor's office again, but this time I was very determined to get my questions answered and have some action taken.

Once more, the same nurse answers my call in a calm, business-like manner. I try to calmly explain to her the critical situation my son is in. I tell her that "there has been no improvement in his color, and his crying and breathing are getting worse." The nurse again calmly answers me, "The doctor says that it should be gone by now" "But it has NOT!!!" I say, raising my voice, "My son is getting worse!" I tell her now with frustration. The nurse sternly tells me to "calm down and says that the doctor will call me once he is done with his other patients," "What!!? You're telling me to calm down and wait! My baby could die right now! I need to see or talk to the doctor now!" I HAVE NO TIME TO WAIT! I WAITED LONG ENOUGH! I WANT TO SPEAK TO THE DOCTOR NOW!

By now, my screams are loud and full of anger. I feel like I'm not being heard or understood by anyone anymore. I have reached my boiling point by now and angrily say: "Lady, I need help now! I don't give a shit what the doctor says. I need help now!" Hearing my tone and my words, the nurse quickly recapitulates a softer tone and says, " I understand you, Mrs. Lopez," then she simply says: *take the baby right away to Children's Hospital on Vermont Street."* "What?" I freeze for a second at what I hear her say. " Take your son to Children's Hospital. They can help you there." She tells me again more polite and helpful manner. "Why didn't you tell me this before?" I tell her in rage. "Why did you wait so long? Why do you do this to us?" I froze in complete shock and anger for a minute. Then I quickly hung up the phone. "Why didn't they say this to me before, I ask repeatedly. Why did they wait so long, and why didn't we think about it before too?" I ask myself again and again in remorse. By now, I feel guilty, lost, and confused about this whole situation.

I walk back to the kitchen, where Xavier is once again crying, and I cannot help but believe that I'm about to have a total meltdown or a nervous breakdown. I know now that my heart has always been right! I say to myself over and over, "This is a nightmare! It can't be happening to us! Something's very wrong with Xavier, and soon I realize I have to compose myself and think of the next step. "I need to take him to Children's Hospital of Los Angeles," and I hear the nurse's words over and over in my head, and I get even angrier. I stop and catch myself and realize that I need to calm down. I must call Jose. I hope that this Hospital could be the place for my son. A place where he could get the help he so desperately needed.

Lord, I Pray!

Chapter 8
Jose gets Home

January 8, 198

Once I pulled myself together, I quickly tried to feed Xavier as best as I could to stop his crying but was unsuccessful. He is in too much discomfort. I call Jose and ask him to come home as soon as possible. I tell him that the baby is in great distress, that he is not eating anymore, and his breathing is shallow. Jose listens to my tone of voice, and without asking anything else, he assures me that he will be rushing home as soon as possible. I then call my mother and mother-in-law to tell them that things are not looking good with the baby. They tell me to try to get a hold of myself to determine the next step. That God is with us and he is in control. We will be praying for you.

"Don't worry about Eddie. He will be fine with us, my mother says. Abuelo is looking forward to his visit." I do not doubt Eddie will be in a good place with them. I'm so grateful for that. "Keep me posted us posted on the situation. We will be praying for you. As I hang up the phone, I come to feel a great sense of fear and loneliness inside me. I now go to Xavier, and both of us, in tears, get ready to go to the hospital. But as I change Xavier's diaper, my whole world suddenly comes tumbling down. I now notice something I had not never before in him. His little body is twitching in short sharp twitches. And even worse, with every twitch, he cries in great discomfort. Seeing this, I, too, begin to cry at the sight of his suffering. I have now become frantic, and I'm having trouble breathing. At this point, I'm glad my mother took Eddie, and he is not here to witness this horrific episode. My thoughts begin to worsen. Being unable to help my son comes with an overwhelming fear of losing him. " He's dying! I think to myself! "My baby is dying!" My crying has become shallow and loud by now. I begin to hyperventilate. I'm losing control of the whole situation. I sit in the bed, hoping not to pass out and leave Xavier alone.

Finally, Jose enters the door and immediately realizes something is terribly wrong with me and the baby! My frail and frantic face said it all. *"Que Pasa,* what's Wong?'' he asks as he quickly but cautiously approaches me, telling me to calm down. "Take deep breaths," he tells me, bringing me a glass of water. I could barely get the words out of my mouth, "He's having seizures!" I tell him, pointing to the baby. I now clearly see the panic on Jose's face too. He quickly gets a hold of himself, trying to be strong for me, and tells me again, "Take deep breaths *mija,* and relax. We are taking the baby to the hospital now!" "Everything will be alright. You'll see. He will be in good hands there." Jose helped me up from the bed, where I sat in dismay. He quickly wraps the baby in a blanket and says, "Here, take the baby. I'll get the diaper bag. We have to get to the hospital right away!" I carefully take Xavier in my arms and try not to look or feel the obvious pain in his body. With each twitch of his little body, my heart bleeds and skips a beat. I tell myself I must be strong and get him to Children's Hospital, where he will finally be helped.

CHAPTER 9
THE DESPERATE DRIVE TO THE HOSPITAL

JANUARY 8, 1982

In our panic, and being so young and inexperienced in these matters, we never think of calling an ambulance to get immediate medical attention for our baby. Instead, we quickly get on the freeway and drive thirty minutes to Children's Hospital in Los Angeles. Somehow we kept getting red lights stopping us, and Jose drove through some of them as safely as he could. Being a truck driver around the city, Jose knew where the Hospital was, and by speeding on the freeway and passing red traffic lights, we finally arrived. Once arriving at the emergency entrance driveway, I quickly get out of the car with my son in my arms. I run towards the emergency entrance calling someone to help me! "Help me! Ayudenme! PLEASE!" 'PLEASE HELP ME."

I can suddenly feel my son's body getting very stiff. I get frantic, and I start screaming even louder for help! HELP ME, PLEASE!!! As I enter the sliding doors of the emergency room, a couple of nurses see me and quickly rush toward me. Within seconds a doctor also runs toward me and immediately sees Xavier's condition. The doctor directly takes Xavier from my arms to the nearest examining room. The nurses now ask me to sit in a small waiting room beside the examining room. They tell me that the doctor will check the baby to see what is happening with him. Scared and not knowing what else to expect or do, I do as they ask me to do. I go to the waiting room to sit. I enter the space and notice the dim lights and cold plastic, rigid gray chairs. Soon Jose dashes into the waiting room and spots me sitting alone in the corner. He quickly walks to my side and asks me about the baby. "A doctor took him, and he is checking him now,"

I tell him between quiet sobs. "The nurses said to wait here until they can find out what is wrong." Jose leans over and holds me tight in his arms. We then begin to pray and cry together in fear of the unknown. So far, this has become a terrifying and painful ordeal for us, and we wonder what else may come our way. It feels like we live in a horrifying "Twilight Zone" episode with no immediate end.

CHAPTER 10
THE QUESTIONS
JANUARY 9, 1982 LATE EVENING

We have been sitting in the cold waiting room for over six hours. The nurses brought in some coffee and blankets for our comfort. It is the early morning of the next day, and we haven't slept a wink, still wondering what is going on with the baby—no news or updates at all this time. Finally, after hours of waiting, a hospital medical team enters the room without the baby. They introduce themselves. "Good morning," they tell us with a slight smile on their faces. "We are the team that will be working with your son." "A team?" I ask. "We will explain ourselves," they say. They quickly introduce themselves as cardiologists, endocrinologists, blood specialists, and pediatric doctors. They informed us that they had some important questions for us to answer as honestly as we could. They ask us to join them on the other side of the waiting room to sit together at a wide round conference table. A nurse sits with us with paper and a pen to take notes. They then turn on the brighter lights in the room to see better.

The team carefully explains that they will ask questions about the baby's birth, hour, date, doctor, and hospital. They also tell us if the baby has been diagnosed with any disease. And that they will be writing everything down for the record.

They begin by saying: "Your son appears to be very sick." They tell us to point blank and right away. And for us to help him and or understand his problems, we need you to answer some critical questions. "Yes, of course," we both agree right away. They tell us that these questions are part of a medical puzzle that they are trying to solve together to help Xavier. "We understand," Jose quickly answers the team.

The endocrinologist then starts with the first set of questions: "Are any of you heavy drug users, or have you been in the past? Are any of you heavy drinkers or smokers? Or have you been in the past?" Our answer is NO to all these questions. "Why are you asking these questions?" I tell them. "Shouldn't we be asking you why my son is twitching?" The cardiologist quickly answers me, "For us to find out about his twitching, we need some critical questions answered by you. As uncommon or unusual as these questions may sound to you, the answers will be beneficial for us to figure out what is going on with your son." "I understand," I answer with resignation. Then more questions continue.

"Have you ever been exposed to any pesticides for a long period? Or have you ever been around Asbestos or any other chemical products for a long time?" "We don't think so," Jose answers. "Does anybody in the immediate family have any congenital disabilities? Most importantly, is anybody in your immediate family born with congenital heart disease?" Again Jose answers no to these questions.

"Where is my son?" I ask anxiously. "Can we see him now? Can I be with him?" The medical team explains, "At the moment, the baby is undergoing a series of important tests and is mostly sedated to help him rest. You can see him when the tests are done. "We have one more question for you." "Did your OBGYN find or tell you there was something suspicious about your pregnancy? Did they find unusual heat rhythms when examining you?" I nervously answered, "No, but most of the time when I went for my monthly or weekly checkups, the heart monitor didn't seem to work." "Who and where is this doctor's hospital or clinic?" They ask. "Dr. Ross, he has a small clinic in East Los Angeles," I answer them. "He also delivered my first son." " Is your first son healthy?" "Yes, he is" I answer him. "Even if the heart monitors were not working, there were other ways to hear the heartbeat. There has to be a good reason why he didn't pursue finding a heartbeat. It's so unusual for a responsible doctor not to do this." This comment breaks my heart and upsets me. And I wonder why I didn't say or do anything about this then. The cardiologist says, "Well, the only thing we have today is the now. The past is gone. We need to see how we can help your son today in the now."

They recommend that it would be better for us and the baby not to be together right now. "That's all our questions for you right now," they say as they get up and shake our hands. "Soon, one of us will return here to talk to you about the test results. Is there any other question you have for us, they ask us?" "No, thank you," Jose answers them. "We don't know what to ask?" The medical team thanks us, and they excuse themselves from the room. The nurse then asks us to sign some papers. When done, Jose and I return and sit quietly in the corner of the room like two scorned children, not knowing what to do, what to think or say. We hold on to each other again while our hearts break into a million pieces. We now wonder what to expect. Our lives have been turned upside down. And we now feel that unfortunately, the worst is yet to come.

CHAPTER 11
THE BAD NEWS

The nurses tell us if we wanted to walk down to the cafeteria and get some coffee or food, it had been a long night, and they didn't know how much longer the test would take. Jose nor I had an appetite, and we decided to keep on waiting. Luckily for us, In less than an hour, two medical team members finally returned to the waiting room with some news.

The cardiologists and the endocrinologists come in the room with somber faces. They once again ask us to join them at the round table on the other side of the room and begin to tell us the news. They start by warning us that they must be honest with us about everything. Jose and I brace ourselves for the report.

Then they start explaining that the results they found in the tests are not good news.

The cardiologist begins by explaining that the results of the heart tests reveal that Xavier was born with a *congenital heart problem* or disease. Hearing these words made my world immediately come crashing down. I can feel pieces of my heart falling bit, by bit to the ground. Then in seconds, I quickly remembered the heart monitors not working during my maternity checkups. What a terrible coincidence! I think to myself.

"His heart condition is called "*Tetralogy of Fallot* " the doctor continues saying. "This is a congenital heart condition or defect due to an abnormal formation of the fetal heart during the first eight weeks of pregnancy. Your obstetrician should have predicted this." Again I think of the broken heart monitor on my maternity checkups. I ask myself again, was this all a terrible, horrifying coincidence?

"Is there anything that can be done for this heart condition?" Jose quickly and frantically asks? "I'm sorry to tell you that this heart condition is unrepairable and unfortunately fatal." By now, I only hear the echoes of the doctor's words and conversation with us. I hear nothing else. And I quickly emerged in my thoughts.

The endocrinologists continue with more bad news. "We also believe that his condition is also part of a syndrome known as **DiGeorge Syndrome** and that, at this moment, we don't know much about this syndrome. We don't have the knowledge or technology how to repair or help these children. Unfortunately, this technology will be available 30 to 40 years from now. But for now, these children are known as "blue babies," and there is very little we can do for them. A syndrome like this means that there may be other complications that come along with this heart condition. In your son's case, his heart and lungs are compromised and very much underdeveloped. His Thymus gland is missing, and he has hypocalcemia or deficient calcium levels, which we believe is causing his spasms or seizures.

"He also has a low immune system and possibly vision problems. All these complications give as a result to be a very short life expectancy for your son. We are so sorry to tell you all this bad news, Mr. and Mrs. Lopez. We wish we had better news for you." At this point, I feel numb and have no energy left in me even to speak. "We understand that this is a lot for you to take in and understand now." Jose and I try to understand or unravel what they just said. It all feels like a complete hell on earth.

" How long does he have to live? " Jose asks. I squeeze his hand, waiting to hear the bad news from the endocrinologist. "Di George babies, because of all their problems, are known to live on the average three to seven weeks at most." My arms and legs go numb again, and once more, I think and feel I'm in a real and horrible Twilight Zone episode.

"This can't be true! This can't be happening to us," I helplessly tell Jose. The doctor replies to my screams, "I'm sorry, Mr. and Mrs. Lopez, these are the test results given to your son. We are so sorry to give such bad news." No! NO POR FAVOR!! I Beg the doctors. I stood up in front of them: "Please help my baby! This cannot be happening to my baby! "PLEASE" I beg of you with all my heart! Tell us it's NOT true!!! I did everything right!" I ate right and saw my doctor regularly! I never felt sick! Please help my son!

Jose gets up to get a hold of me to calm me down. My frantic reaction scares him. But soon, he, too, breaks down with me and cries. The doctors, wanting to give us privacy, quickly excuse themselves from the room. And now, for us, our nightmare begins. We hold each other tight. Our tears blend as one in our faces. We feel like we're in another world now, lost and all alone. We now realize that our nightmare is absolute and real! We are in the Lord's hands now. Jose and I are left alone in a cold, dark waiting room, holding on to each other as one with God.

Chapter 12
Living in Children's Hospital

January 29, 1982

Living in a hospital with my son for almost three weeks is difficult and draining for me and anyone. We hoped that by now, we would be done with this whole ordeal, but there is no sign of when or how this ordeal will be over. Our world, as we knew it once, has clashed so rapidly down a deep drain. We now know that whatever change is coming will not be for the better but for the worst. Whether ready or not, or whether we accept it or not, death is coming!

Living inside a hospital like this, with a sick child for so long, means not knowing whether it's day or night or even what day of the week or month is in the outside world. A world that doesn't seem to know you even exist. Hospital lighting is the same twenty-four hours a day, seven days a week. Unless you're lucky to be near a window, days and hours seem to blend in and have no real meaning here.

With Jose back to work, my weekdays and nights alone in the hospital are spent sitting by my son's crib. My hospital metal chair becomes very uncomfortable after a few hours in the same position. I am always by Xavier's side and do not pay attention or care about my discomfort. In keeping a constant watch on my son's monitors, I have come to learn how to read them and understand numbers and their meanings. This is what I do when Xavier sleeps. I ask many questions and read whatever article, magazine, or book on DiGeorge Syndrome that the nurses kindly bring for me to read. I want to know everything written about this matter. The nurses say that I will probably earn a medical degree with all the questions and research I do. Since the doctors only gave my son weeks to live, I try every day and every minute to keep my son somehow comfortable and alive a bit longer. I try to take advantage of what little time he sleeps and rest a bit at a time.

Some good news I see is that Xavier has almost passed the first three weeks of life expectancy, and I hope for more. The doctors tell me that most Di-George syndrome babies don't usually live this long and are surprised that Xavier is gaining a little weight. I know very clearly that death is inevitable and that my son is condemned to have a very short life, but I am determined to keep him alive as much as possible. I know and feel that always being at his side helps him be tranquil and his heart and lungs at peace by not crying. This allows him to stay out of the crisis. I somehow know in my heart and soul this to be true.

I have by now become accustomed to the hospital noise, lighting, and lifestyle. I have become better familiar with his team of doctors and nurses. I ask many questions and get many answers, all of which help me figure out what is happening with my son. The doctors tell me they have never met a mother like me. One who is so young, never giving up, and always looking for answers to help her son. I find this journey very difficult, but I need some control to survive all this.

Without Jose or any or the family by my side in the hospital during the week, my life is very lonely in this emotional prison. Both my son and I are locked in this hospital cage, waiting for the inevitable end. Praying and holding him in my arms comforts both him and I. We are bonding deeper and deeper every day. It's getting harder for me to let him go. I plan to stay with him as long as I can, no matter how physically exhausting It becomes for me. I sleep and eat very little, and even little everyday things like showers are less frequent.

Jose and many family members visit us during the weekends. This gives me great comfort and joy and the energy to continue. I haven't been home for weeks now. Since Eddie is so young, he cannot come to the hospital room to see Xavier. My sister often brings Eddie downstairs to the waiting room where I can have "mommy son" time. I miss Eddie so much. I feel lucky to have my family take care of him during this time. I know his little heart wonders what is happening in the grown-up world. Why doesn't he see Mommy and Daddy every day at home like before? I also speak to him on the phone at times, and he always asks me about Xavier and when he will be going home. His innocent words tear at my heart, and I don't know how to answer him. I only tell him that I miss him and that I love him very much.

CHAPTER 13
TRANSLATIONS

FEBRUARY 10, 1982

The hospital is a very frightening and depressing place for babies and parents. I never thought that such a place ever existed. And much less. I never thought that I would be living here with a sick child. I have witnessed many awful and heartbreaking situations in my many weeks living here. I have seen many kinds of illnesses and diseases, some of which I have never heard of. I have woken up to crying babies and empty cribs where there was a baby. I have seen new babies (patients) arriving at all times of the day or night, I'm not sure. I have witnessed the parent's pain and helplessness upon seeing their child's suffering. I know this myself too well.

I have come to see children being left alone in the hospital by their parents or family members. I especially feel bad for these children, for they suffer a terrible illness and a great loss for not having anyone by their side. At first, I came to question and judge these parents' and families' insensitive hearts. But I soon realized and learned these parents have many reasons and circumstances for doing so. Not all parents have the luxury that I have of having a supporting family and husband who support me one hundred percent. Jose's job is financially stable, and my family cares for Eddie.

I now have come to realize that some parents depend on two incomes to keep their livelihood. Others with more children have no support system or no one to watch their children stay in the hospital with their sick children. I even met some single mothers who are all alone in raising their children, and of course with no support system. Whatever the case, this place is very difficult for families of sick children to live in.

There have been many times when the nurses have asked me to translate into Spanish for non-English speaking families. The bad part of translating is that I give the parents mostly bad and tragic news about their sick children. This has become very difficult for me. This hospital wing hosts the "Terminally ill Children." And translating news here is never good or pleasant.

For example, Mr. and Mrs. Perez have come onto the floor with a two-year-old little girl named Cindy, who has been diagnosed with terminal stage four Leukemia. I had a hard time explaining to these parents that there was nothing else the doctors could do for their little daughter. Mrs. Perez begged me to ask the doctors for a miracle. I wished to translate a more positive answer for them, but I had no other than bad news.

Living in this place, at times, I have seen little body bags being wheeled out in the hallways in the middle of the night. Like a revolving door, I see new baby patients, along with their tormented parents and families, come to this floor as what seems to me to be like a "mouse trap." A place where your child may never get out alive. Witnessing these parents' first arrival reminds me of the day Jose and I walked in through those doors with our sick son, feeling lost and broken. Although the doctors and nurses are very kind and helpful here, it's still tough to be here. I honestly don't know how the people working here handle all this. I now sit praying and thinking about why things like this happen. Why does God allow them? But I know deep in my heart that God has a reason for all this, and so I mostly pray for understanding, patience, and acceptance.

In this horrible place, I also think a lot about my Eddie. I wonder how he is doing? I wonder how this ordeal will affect him now and in the future. I know that both my sons need me, and I need them. I'm torn between living here in the hospital or going home to Eddie. Sometimes when I wake up from a brief sleep, I open my eyes, hoping that this hospital disappears, that it's nothing but a long bad dream, and that I'm home with my two boys. But I soon realize that my situation here is authentic, and I still live an absolute nightmare.

CHAPTER 14
VALENTINES DAY

Today is Valentine's Day. I only know this because of the decorations in the nurse's stations. The hallways are decorated with red cupids shooting little pink and red hearts. I have seen Xavier undergo many painful tests and lengthy procedures this week, all giving the same dreadful results. "There is nothing that can help him." I wish that this Valentine's Day would be a miracle for my son. A day when my son can rest and not be tortured by needles.

Valentine's Day to me right now means nothing much. Jose is planning to come to visit us. He gave this message to the nurse, whom we have come to know so well by now. Being a Wednesday, Jose's day off, he can spend the evening with us. Every time Jose visits us, it's short, and it gets harder and harder for Xavier and me to say goodbye to him. We have not been together for more than an hour for so long. I do miss him, and I know he misses me. It will be so nice to have him here for more than an hour on Valentine's Day.

Jose comes into the room with a small bouquet for me. It's so lovely to see him. His embrace is warm and tender. I want it to last forever. This is my real Valentine's present. He then goes over and picks up Xavier in his arms. "Hello, little buddy," he tells him. All three of us embraced, Jose said Happy Valentine's Day, and for more than three hours, it was all so wonderful. The only person missing from our circle was Eddie. Our Valentine's circle of love was not complete, but it was nice to have.

I speak to Eddie on the phone daily, but it's not enough. I need to hold, kiss and put him in his bed to sleep. Besides Xavier's condition, not having to see Eddie is also heavy in my heart.

Happy Valentine's day the nurses say as they pass the hallway and stick their heads in the room to greet us. For a few hours, my Valentine's present is here in the present. My husband and son are by my side. Other than having Eddie here, I desire nothing else for now. For a few hours, it is all some sort of state of some kind of "normality," giving us the strength to continue living our lives and our reality. Happy Valentines.

CHAPTER 15
LITTLE GABRIEL
MARCH 2, 1982

One sunny day in March, Xavier gets a little roommate named Gabriel. The nurse shares with me that Gabriel has Down syndrome and severe heart, and lung complications and will be sharing the room with Xavier. She tells me that his mother is a teenage single mother, who says can't handle little Gabriel's condition. She has given him up for adoption at the hospital. Right away I begin to feel a sort of deep and maternal love for this sweet little boy. The fact that his mother will not be here to hold him breaks my heart. "Little Gabriel's mother is too young to understand," the nurse tells me, "and doesn't know how to deal with a sick baby at home." "I feel bad for little Gabriel already," I tell the nurse as a technician comes in to draw blood from Gabriel and hears my comment.

The nurse tenderly holds Gabriel's hand and talks to him as his little arm as the technician's long needles draw blood from his little arm. Gabriel then begins to cry. By now I am holding Xavier in my arms, preventing him from crying. " Xavier is so lucky to have you, Mrs. Lopez." the nurse tells me as she tries to console Gabriels crying. "Having the moms here helps babies cope with all that happens to them here." The blood technician joins the conversation and says, "In my 17-year experience in this wing, I have found that the babies that get personal love and attention tend to respond a little better to medications and live a bit longer than those left alone." "I never thought about this," I told them. I guess we are one of the lucky ones. "Yes, you are," the tech tells me as he warmly touches my shoulder. "You are here for a reason other than your son. I'm sure of that," He says as he leaves the room. "I agree with him," the nurse says. "One day, you will come to understand all this, and you will be able to help others like you if you're not already doing it. It's all so unfortunate and tragic. I assure you that God makes no mistakes."

By now, little Gabriel has quieted down and, with his little pacifier, is fast falling asleep in his metal crib. Now I sit with my son across the room, looking at us in the mirror. I look tired and worn out. I see myself holding on to my child, who seems and feels like an extension of me at this time. At this point, I'm unsure if I'm holding on to him or if he is holding on to me. We seem to be an extension of one another.

A Message to Mama from Xavier

You are me and I am you

The same blood, the same heart

In everything we do

We are one

That's what was meant to be

We are together now, mama

And in heaven, we will be too

An extension of me is YOU

To Mama from Xavier

CHAPTER 16
LIVING WITH LITTLE GABRIEL
MARCH 9, 1982

Little Gabriel's crib is a few feet from Xavier's crib. He is a quiet baby, never making a fuss. Now that Xavier is sleeping and Gabriel is awake, I walk over to see him. As always he right away greets me with a big smile. I can't help but extend my arms over to him to pick him up. He is a bit older than my son and it always feels good to hold him. He usually first stares at me and looks at my face repeatedly with curiosity. His little hands begin to touch my face and quickly explore my features. I feel that this is his way of telling me he likes me. Then, as I walk him around the room, he takes full interest in his surroundings. The pictures on the wall of baby animals are his favorite to see and touch. He likes his walks out in the hallways and smiles at everyone passing by. "You're a little angel," they say as they pass him.

When Xavier first met his little roommate, they quickly became good friends. Little Gabriel has grown fond of my visits to his crib and of bringing Xavier over to play sit with him. At times Gabriel can hold himself up with the bars in his bed and demand my attention. I find it amusing, and little Gabriel somehow knows it too. Days go by and the three of us form a sort of little family together. I'm so glad I could be part of Gabriel's life as long as I can. At times Gabriel sits inside Xavier's crib and Xavier seems to like that. The two little friends seem to communicate in their very own language. I love to see them together, keeping each other company, happy, and content in a place such as this. It's impressive to see how well they seem to know each other, perhaps from another life. At times they seem and act like old friends. They look and "coo" to each other with some sort of whimsical language and understanding of their situations and each other. I find it amazing, and I'm not sure why or how, but I somehow seem to understand it all. Babies seem to share this magical spirit, something we adults come to lose or forget as we age.

I feel so blessed that my son has his little friend. And I also feel happy that Gabriel shares my son's room and that he is not alone.

Chapter 17
The First Real Goodbye

APRIL 13, 1982

Today I woke up from napping in my chair, and as always, holding Xavier's little hand in mine. I wake and look at Xavier, who is tranquil and comfortably sleeping, and come to notice that little Gabriel is not in his crib. This worries me because I had to stay away from Gabriel for a couple of days because he has a bad cough and runny nose, and I wonder if not being in his crib has anything to do with that.

Before my son wakes, I decide to go out to the hallway nurse station and ask about Gabriel. The nurse informed me that little Gabriel has developed a high fever and had been taken to the ICU for observation. I'm apprehensive about him now. He has been our little roommate for many weeks, and Xavier and I have grown fond of him. Because I know that there's nobody here for him but me and the nurses. I'm thinking I can go to the ICU to see him and see how I can help him. I don't think it's a good idea, the nurse quickly answers me. I don't need to remind you that your son is also very sick and he needs you there. Besides, you don't want to risk bringing anything back from the ICU to your son. I guess you're right, I told the nurse. I sadly returned to my son's room. You don't need to worry about Gabriel, Mrs. Lopez. The nurse says as she follows me to the room. "Save your time, worry, and energy for your son, which I know you will need."

Needless to say that little Gabriel holds a special place in my heart, so I begin to pray for him. Something tells me that little Gabriel isn't doing well. He has not been his happy self in the last two days. He has been sad and in much discomfort. He just hasn't been his usual cheerful self.

Many hours pass, and little Gabriel has not returned to the room. With Xavier sleeping in my arms, the nurse comes in with his dinner. I ask her then about Gabriel's condition. "Gabriel has a bad infection in his lungs and heart," she tells me. "And unfortunately, it's not looking good for him now. I feel numb with this sad news.

   That afternoon when Xavier had his medications and was now comfortably sleeping. I decide to go to the ICU Unit and try to see Gabriel, at least from a faraway window. I know the nurse there from having Xavier in the ICU many times before, and I'm hoping it will help me. "What are you doing here, Mrs. Lopez?" A nurse suddenly startles me from behind the window. "How is he doing?" I ask with hand signals through the thick glass window. At the moment he is on a respirator. She answers me through a small speaker on the side of the window. She then slides the whole heavy curtain to one side so I can see little Gabriel completely through the thick glass. I now see him with tubes taped to his face and body. I realize that things are worse than I thought. The nurse then says that she will allow me to stay by the window for a couple of minutes. " I get closer to the window." My heart hurts with this scene. Somehow I know that this is the last time I'm going to see him. "Goodbye little angel, you're going to rest and live in heaven now. There is no illness or pain in heaven, my little friend, I say as I bless him and send him a kiss." I stood there in quiet tears, looking at him behind the curtain for a few minutes. The nurse then asks me to please leave the unit. That my time with Gabriel was up. I thank The nurse for letting me see him one last time and head back to my son's room.

Getting back to my son's room, I picked him up from his crib and into my arms in the consolation of what I had just witnessed. I hold Xavier even tighter and closer to my heart in a blanket of tears. Now more than ever, I realize that death is coming. It's right around the corner. Xavier's eyes and quiet spirit tell me that he somehow, in some way, understands all that's going on.

Today has been a very long day, and now at night, I sit in my chair holding my son in my arms, trying to sleep. I stare at Gabriel's empty crib. I am not looking forward to receiving bad news about him. Either way, one can never be ready for death.

It's morning, and the bad news comes early. I am told that little Gabriel passed just a few hours ago. I cry from the deepest part of my soul. Holding Xavier in my arms is soothing, and in his little face, I could see he will miss his little friend too. Little Gabriel is gone to heaven now, I whisper to his little ear. He's an angel now. Xavier's eyes look straight into my eyes, and he speaks love to me.

SMALL LITTLE HEARTS

Small little hearts, inside cold metal, cribs

Needles and tubes tearing their

little hands, heads, and feet

Little bodies tremble in fear

Feeling attacked by masked giants in green

Some will be dying at night in their metal beds

As they sleep

Rooms filled with crying babies and medicine machines

Hanging from metal poles, these decorate the scenes

Small little hearts needing love and warmth

To live for a bit more

then they are gone

Then an Angel they'll be

For little Gabriel 4/82

CHAPTER 18
XAVIER IN THE ICU

JUNE 7, 1982

It is very early this morning and after a long agonizing night of fever and pain, my son has been quickly transferred to the ICU. He has been gone now for over four hours. All I know is that he is getting some critical tests done. I can't help but worry about my son's well-being and for being gone so long from me. Not having a Thymus gland added more problems for my baby. His immune system is declining. And to make things worse, the doctors have found that his little body is not producing enough calcium to sustain his bone structure safely. Because of this, his convulsions are getting worse.

The endocrinologist finally arrives at the waiting room where Jose and I sit waiting once and for evermore. He brings unfortunate news. He informs us that Xavier is convulsing too frequently now in the examining room. And they are trying, through some tests, to figure out how to help him. He continues telling us that it doesn't look good. He recommends we call the family and be ready for the inevitable end. Soon our families come and join us for support. My mother-in-law sits by me, telling me that the baby is in God's hands.

By now two ICU nurses come to inform us that again the baby is not responding to phenobarbital, and he is still dangerously convulsing. My mother and mother-in-law begin to pray. The family tries to console us and give us hope. By now, the whole family began to pray the rosary. Everyone is expecting the worst at any minute now. By now, I'm feeling faint and disoriented. The long days and weeks in the hospital begins to take a toll on me. She's having an emotional breakdown, my sister says, as she fans some air on my face. This is too much for her, my father says

Jose sits by my side with some wet paper towels and places them on my forehead. It takes a few minutes for me to slowly recover from this small crisis. I'm here, Jose tells me. The family is here with us. We are not alone in this. Just about this time, the endocrinologist returns to the room where the family anxiously awaits news. He announces that the baby, by some miracle, is slowly responding to a new medication. "We are waiting to see if it will stay on his body and stop the convolutions." "We have to wait and see. We hope and pray that it will work," the doctor says as he leaves the room, leaving us with hope.

"It's incredible and a miracle!" The doctor says as he returns to the room a half hour later. "Xavier has finally responded to his new treatment. His convulsions have stopped for now." "You can see him in about an hour when he returns to his room." The whole family responds with hugs and cries of gratitude and thankfulness to God and the Blessed Mother (Guadalupe). And continues praying. Jose and I are in tears hoping Xavier is, at least for now, out of immediate danger.

I tell myself that this is a trial practice for what will soon come. Unfortunately, this was a dress rehearsal for the event we all dreadfully wait for. A bad taste stays in my mouth for now, something I had not had before. I wonder if it's the taste of death?

CHAPTER 19
XAVIER'S DOWN SPIRAL

JULY 10, 1982

After losing little Gabriel, my son's hospital room has become even more cloudy, dark, and gloomy. We needed Gabriel's little smile to light up the room and keep us company. In all these weeks, I can feel my son's sadness, I see it in his eyes. I know it's because of little Gabriel's absence. It's like he somehow knows it will soon be his turn to go to heaven.

After our BIG scare in the ICU, I try to be uplifting for my baby boy. I take him for long walks in the hallways as he likes and, whenever possible, walk him to the hospital's little garden at the top of the third floor. But nothing seems the same for him, even me, without our little friend. Through the following weeks, Xavier's thrive was not as strong as before. His breathing became increasingly complex, and his color darker in tone. My heart was breaking into little pieces, and I only knew how bad. Jose and the family visit on the weekends, but I never leave the baby's site for no reason. Not knowing when his last breath will be, I just stay by his side.

In these last weeks, I have witnessed Xavier's downward spiral. The doctors warn me once more to be strong and be ready for the inevitable. Jose has asked for days off to be with us. This helps me. Xavier's seizures are coming back. The calcium levels continue helplessly dropping. Jose and I feel lost once more and wonder if he will return to the ICU soon or, even worse, die now.

July 13, 1982

A few days later, we were pleasantly surprised to see Xavier a bit better on Monday morning. Although he is still blue, his face color seems a little more lively. His daily routine checkup team is also somewhat impressed and surprised to see Xavier with a certain glow about him. When the cardiologist sees him, he quickly recommends taking advantage of this small window of luck to do an intervention and help his lungs breathe better. I question whether the doctor will have Xavier go to this procedure safely. I know it requires some form of anesthesia, which could be deadly to Xavier. The cardiologist admits that it's a risk, but he feels Xavier has been deteriorating in the last weeks and feels this chance might be worth taking to have him live a little longer.

Jose and I also see Xavier a bit more responsive, and even the nurses are happy to see his appearance. Jose and have a few minutes to think about the doctor's recommendation. After thinking and praying we decided to go through with the "shunt" procedure, hoping and praying to give him a bit more time with us.

July 14, 1982

Very early the very next morning the nurses prepare Xavier for the minor surgery. Jose and I have mixed emotions and feelings. As the operating nurse comes in to take him, it is our time to bless him and kiss him goodbye. I trust the doctors, and I am letting God do his will, but my heart somehow knew that by not being by his side after waking from the surgery, Xavier would panic and be in great danger of dying. After begging and asking the doctors and nurses to let me be in the recovery room when my son awakes, I was repeatedly denied access.

The procedure was done in less than two hours. The news came to us that it had gone well and that Xavier was in the recovery room waiting to wake. I again beg to be allowed with my son in the recovery room. I told them I needed to be there when he woke so he could see me and not panic and cry. This is crucial! I tell them that I've never left his sight before and that I know not seeing me by him will kill him. Again they denied access and told me that they knew what they were doing and that it would all be alright, that there were plenty of nurses in the recovery room for him. "But it's not the same!" I tell them in desperation. But still, I am denied.

At this point, I feel I'm abandoning my child, as other mothers have done. How could I allow this to happen? I have never left my son's side. Something bad was going to happen, I knew! Jose tries calming me down, saying I did not abandon Xavier. That I am a good mother and that he and everyone know that. But that doesn't seem to help me, and I soon come to realize that the circumstances, in this case, are far beyond my control and possibly tragic.

Xavier is finally brought to his room. I could tell something was terribly wrong with him! First of all, I could tell he was left alone crying for a while. His little tormented face showed me his fright. The obvious was that he was suffocating. His little mouth opened wide, trying to catch more air. His little chest was rising, and his color was grayish blue by this time again. "You let him cry! That's what happened. You left him alone to cry!" I yelled at the nurses trying to help his breathing, but they were unsuccessful.

I wanted to pick him up and take him in my arms, and I was then told not to pick him up until his Iv was done. I am in agony, the same agony my son is in. Jose tries to calm me down, but he knows something is so wrong. Even the cardiologist stepping in the room, once seeing the situation, gave an impression of great concern.

The four walls in the room seem to be caving in. I am losing touch with my reality, I know my son is dying. He is leaving me slowly, I can tell. "Help him. Please help him!" I anxiously beg the doctor, but he just looks back at me, confirming my worst nightmare. My baby left me that night.

I Held My Baby Through The Night

I held my baby through the night

Before he left and said goodbye

I was alone and now I see

I had the privilege to see him free

Free from the pain so harsh and tearing

Free from this earth to walk in heaven

He said goodbye with just a sigh

In me, he lived for just a while

He went and left a painful token

Too sad to see my heart was broken

I knew I had to say goodbye

The day I was away from you my son

The night you left was short

as short ....as your life

July 14, 1982

July 18, 1982

The Funeral

I always knew this day would come—my son's final goodbye. I sit at home in full denial, resisting to face the reality of what waited for me at the funeral home. My sister patiently sits beside me. Everyone, including Jose, has already gone to the funeral home. But I refuse to go. After a few minutes, II suddenly feel an urge and painful emotions come over me. Desperate NOT to leave my son alone at the funeral home, I finally begged my sister to drive me there. My sister had not even parked the car when I got out and ran to the funeral home's front door. When entering, I immediately see my son's little white coffin in the center of a well-lid altar. Everyone heard my cry and immediately turned back to see me. I'm not sure how I finally got to him, but when I finally did, I went down on my knees with unbearable sorrow.

I knew that it would be hard to see him in his little coffin. Jose and my sisters now sit in the front row with me, trying to console me. More friends and family sit behind us in support. I feel fortunate to have people that love us by our side. My father stands brokenhearted in the backside of the funeral home, holding Eddie. He is far away from the coffin, mainly staying on the patio, protecting Eddie from the viewing.

At this moment, I feel that no one but Jose really knows of my deepest feelings. A feeling that only parents who lose a child can understand. Even if surrounded by people, I feel so alone and misunderstood by most. Even if people mean well by saying, "I'm sorry for your loss," they are just words to me right now.

Seeing some family and friends attending the service with their little ones has been especially difficult. With good intentions, some pay their respects to Jose and me, holding their child in their arms. The worst part is seeing those infants hover over mine, like a spectacle, in his tiny coffin. Thoughts rush through my mind. What's the point of parents doing this? Why bring their children to a time like this? Why bring them to the coffin? I suppose this is something that no one ever thinks can be painful for me and Jose to see right now.

What I do know is that everyone in attendance is people that care and love us. This means a lot to us. This is when I come to realize that in these painful moments, we really need friends and family around us the most. I now know that the people here love us unconditionally. Today I realize how much love we have around us.

In contrast, I also realize I miss those people who didn't come and whom I thought I could count on and be present at a time like this. The service and the goodbye was already difficult enough with out them.

IF YOU HAD COME

I REALLY THOUGHT YOU WOULD COME

TO BE WITH ME ON THIS

DREADFUL TERRIBLE DAY OF MINE

I LOOKED AROUND FOR YOU

BUT YOU WERE NOT THERE

YOU DIDN'T COME

SURROUNDED BY PEOPLE

I NEEDED YOU HERE

AND I DONT UNDERSTAND WHY

YOU DIDN'T COME

.........YET I DO NOW

CHAPTER 20
AFTER XAVIER'S DEATH

JULY 28, 1982

It has been two weeks since my son went to live in heaven. His little heart and lungs were too weak to continue living. He tried hard to stay, but it was too difficult for him to breathe towards the end. He left in the middle of the night as I held him and sang his favorite songs to him. Like always, his little hand held onto my small finger for reassurance. Little by little, I felt his spirit leaving his body until he took his last breath, and his little hand went cold. In losing him, I lost half of my heart. He and I were like one. We were inseparable. Doctors said that was what kept my son alive all this time. For almost seven months, I never left his side. Not to eat or sleep. I don't like to think or talk about my life with him in the hospital or about how he died in my arms. It's too painful. And now I have to adjust to living a life without him.

I sometimes wonder if I could have done more to save him. Should we have done more to keep him alive longer? Did we make a mistake in allowing the difficult procedure to happen? "If only, If only," I say over and over, but then soon realize that the past is gone, that my son is gone, and we have a new empty life without him.

Chapter 21
A Broken Soul
August 25, 1982

Since my son's death, I find it very difficult to even breathe. I miss holding his little hand in mine. Hours and days go by, and I lay on the sofa all day staring at the living room window in silence. Every part of my being hurts, from my hair to my nails. I have no more tears left inside me. I feel like my insights are torn to pieces. I somehow manage to drive daily to the cemetery, not knowing how I get there. I visit his grave every day and sit there for hours, not saying a word, just thinking about our time together. Then I go home, where I feel that nothing else exists. My son and husband are the only people I know who are keeping me alive. Both are worried about me. Especially Jose. He has taken up drinking to erase his pain. That, too, scares me.

My parents have taken Eddie to their home for a few days now. I know I'll have Eddie back when I feel better. And I hope that it will be soon. For now, everything and every day seem gray. The colors of life are gone. Nothing makes absolute sense to me anymore. I see the worry and pain in Jose's eyes, and I am not happy with him starting to drink again. I know it's his way of coping. When he gets home after work, and finds me in the same place he left me in the morning. With nothing on the stove, the house is a mess, and I am not caring about anything. He heads for the refrigerator for a beer. This is not him or me at all! It's not who we really are. I can't seem to have the energy to get back to who I was before all this, and I don't know how to do it anymore. Jose is coping with what he can in order to continue working and providing for his family. We walk around the house like two lost and broken people and have become in a way, two total strangers.

I need help. I need someone who understands me. I feel so all alone. I need to feel loved and, most of all cared for. Where is everybody, I ask? They are all carrying out their everyday lives. I feel I'm left out and left behind. Jose does his best, but I need more. My love "well" is empty. I gave it all away. This is when I wish I had someone like me around. No one's world has stopped but mine and Jose's. Everyone else is riding the merry-go-round of life and has forgotten us. At least, that's how I feel right now. The people I thought would spend time with me don't come. I feel that the world goes on without me. I'm so out of touch.

Chapter 22
I'm Dying

Today, Jose came home from work and found me once more sleeping in the middle of the floor in the middle of the day. "Why are you on the floor again?" "Why didn't you go out with your sisters for lunch as we agreed?" Looking back at him, I could see the deep worry for me in his eyes. He knows I'm dying inside. He helps me get off the floor and to the sofa. He holds my hands close to him and tells me. " I'm so worried about you. We need professional help to get through this, *mija.* So much has happened to us in less than a year. Anybody who has gone through what we did would feel the same."

"We can do this together. I know we can. But I can't do it alone. I worry about you not caring for yourself scares me. You are suffering from some deep depression, I'm sure of that." "I realize that I must be the strong one to keep sane and seek help for both of us. We owe this to Eddie" He says, " I don't want to continue drinking. I want to stop before it gets worst or out of hand."

"One thing that crosses my mind, he tells me": "I spoke with my mother, and she has agreed to come from San Francisco where she lives with my older brother, to spend some days with us and hopefully help you. She has always been very caring with you, and I'm sure her company will help you understand many things. I agreed with Jose's advice and I knew that my mother-in-law was a wise and loving woman and that she somehow would be good to my soul. I've been told that she has gone through some tragedies and grown to be a compassionate and understanding woman. She is no stranger to death. She has had many losses, two of them being young children.

Losing a child marks you for life, and no one else understands a mother's mourning but another mother who has had losses. I knew of my mother-in-law's losses but I never thought I would be one of the mothers who would have to go through this journey. The journey of losing half of your heart and soul. I believe this is one of the most painful paths in a woman's journey through life. " I know I need help. I know I'm dying, and I need to stay alive!" I need someone like my mother-in-law.

CHAPTER 23
MY MOTHER IN LAW:
DOMITILA

SEPTEMBER 2, 1982

Jose arranged for my mother-in-law to stay with us for a few days. Her name is Maria Domitila and she was born and lived most of her life in the village of La Laja. She brought with her the teas and herbs from her home village. She says these teas will help me feel better. After a warm hello, she immediately goes to the kitchen and begins boiling water for tea. While the water boils, she begins freshening up the kitchen by opening the windows and washing and putting dishes away. I sit on the sofa as I have been for the last few weeks. She is numb and un- attentive to what she sees, but I know she understands my emotional and physical state based on her mannerisms. With a cup of manzanilla and *canela* tea, she comes to sit with me on the sofa. Before she begins her conversation, she asks me to slowly sip the tea and relax. Then she tells me a story about her *comadre* Sofia's little five-year-old daughter, who tragically died from a spider bite back in her home village of La Laja.

At first, I wasn't sure why she was telling me this sad story, but when she continued, I realized what her goal was. She told me how Sofia's only child suffered for three days and nights with a very high fever due to that spider's dreadful bite. She herself witnessed the little girl's body fighting the poison. No medical service was nearby, which made the situation even more tragic. Sofia cried and prayed for her daughter to get well and recover. The whole village tried to help her by also praying and taking her herbs to possibly help her little girl.

After a day and night of severe fever and paralyzing pain, Sofia's little girl dies. "Soon after that, my *comadre* Sofia fell into deep dissolution and depression." She tells me that "Sofia's only child was gone." "Her world was torn to pieces. She blamed herself for not cleaning her small shack well enough to find the spider before it got to her daughter." "Her husband took on drinking and was never home for Sofia. In fact, he blamed Sofia for the little girl's death and for not being a caring mother."

"One early morning, Sofia, wrongly feeling guilty for her daughter's death, went to the highest point of the river bank and purposely threw herself into the high current. She was never seen alive again. Her pain was too deep to keep on living. She hoped that in dying and in leaving this life, she would somehow get to see and be with her little girl again."

Afterward, with what happened to Sofia that dreadful day, my mother-in-law continued, "The women in the village felt guilty for not knowing how to help her and for not staying by her side day and night and reassuring her it wasn't her fault. We wished we would have been there for her at the time she needed help dealing with her r doubts and agonizing self-inflicted guilt. We felt we left her alone too soon, for too long. We wondered if we did enough to help her save her life?"

"From Sofia's terrible tragedy we, the women of the village, made an honor pledge to always be there for one another, especially when mourning the death of a child." One can easily lose your mind over the loss of a child. "Nothing could be worse than that mija. I know how you feel, I myself lost two infants." Now looking straight into my eyes she says, "I am here for you. And so are the women in the village who are already praying for you at this time. I want you to know that you are not alone."

"You are walking a dark road of mourning right now, as many women have before you, but please know that with time, the sun will shine in your life again." "Let us hold on to one of your hands, and let God take you by the other. "He and the Blessed Mother will walk you out of this darkness." "Everything that happens in our lives teaches us a valuable lesson. I know it may not make sense to you right now, but this whole ordeal will make you stronger later on *mija. And you will fully understand when it's time and you're ready for it. God doesn't make mistakes.* Now drink your tea, it will make you feel better and it will help you sleep."

I spend many mornings and evenings like this, talking and listening to more stories from my mother-in-law's village and life experiences. Listening to her stories help me get through my day. Through these stories, I have come to learn much. I slowly feel a bit of the grayness disappearing from my life, and begin to see some colors. During this time, Eddie has come back home and I am now somewhat able to pay more attention to his needs. Eddie definitely brings back colors in my life.

After spending days with my mother-in-law, she tells me that she has to return to her home in San Francisco and promises to return soon. She leaves with me the stories and her wise words to think about. I feel that these weeks have significantly made an impact on me. I will always be grateful to her for this. I now try to take one day at a time, as she says. I have moments of sadness and bad flashbacks of the hospital, but I'm now learning to return from these memories more easily. My mother-in-law is a wise woman. Her stories gave me the strength to keep moving forward.

CHAPTER 24
EDDIE
SEPTEMBER 2, 1982

Eddie is a loving and understanding little boy with a big heart. He has been a real trooper for me and his father throughout this ordeal. He, too, is another of my sweet angels. I feel complete with him in my life. Eddie is a big help to my emotional needs. When I'm with him, I feel so much joy. The joy makes me feel like I have both my sons with me. I can tell that Eddie is also feeling much more relaxed around me too, now that some of my tension is beginning to alleviate our situation.

He, too, likes being with his grandmother and father. He has a somewhat normal life there. He gets all the attention he needs and wants and sometimes even more. Now that I spent some time living with my mother-in-law, I can tell he senses the peace coming over me and his father. Eddie has begun sharing his little stories about his "Ninja Turtle" adventures and his love for Batman. He loves to role-play and he always includes us in his stories. I love seeing him like this, he definitely fills a void in my heart.

Jose is also glad to have Eddie home and see me finally taking a step forward. He too is now getting help with his drinking. "We are not out of the woods yet," he tells me, "but we are on your way there." "I love to see you and Eddie so happy together. This means a lot to me and my own healing." "Your words mean a lot to me," I tell him as I kiss him and he kisses Eddie and me back.

Eddie, Jose, and I are trying to slowly recover and live our lives as a family now. Our routine is almost back to normal. We have breakfast together, and in the afternoon we go to play in the park as we did before. After dinner, he plays with Jose, and at the end of the day, Jose takes him a bath. At bedtime, I read Eddie his favorite bedtime story. Sometimes we all cuddle in bed to a good movie.

Chapter 25
The Diaper Bag
September 8,1982

Today I dropped Eddie off to play with his little cousins so that I could do my daily visit to the cemetery. When I returned home, I found a large box on my front door steps. The box is from "The Children's Hospital of Los Angeles". At first, I didn't think much of it, until I saw a note attached to it that read: *"To the parents of Xavier Lopez."* I pull the note from the box and begin to reread it closely. The sentence at the bottom of the message says: Xavier's diaper bag was found in the hospital warehouse. The hospital apologized for the inconvenience, and it is now being returned to me.

At first, I was baffled. I forgot that this diaper bag even existed anymore. With all that happened, I had no idea it had been left behind in the hospital. And now it's here at my front door inside this box. I stood on the front porch for a few minutes. I read the note over and over. It took a while for me to decide whether to pick up the box and take it inside the house with me or leave it on the porch until Jose got home.

I choose to take it inside the house. Once inside the house, I place it on top of the dining room table. I think of not opening it until Jose gets home, but my curiosity and seeing the diaper bag overtake me. This feeling starts to be stronger than me. I now realize that I'm glad my sister had Eddie to spend the day with her kids. I wouldn't want him to see me have some kind of bad reaction to this package.

Having the diaper bag here once more at home makes my heart race and my hands sweaty. I walk and sit on the living room sofa. I'm trying to take control of myself and not look towards the table where the box sits, but still, I can't help wanting to see the contents in the bag again. With no time to think anymore, I suddenly get an urge to go to the table and finally open the box. I'm not sure if it is a good idea to do so without Jose, but my thoughts are racing back and forth in my head. Should I? Or shouldn't I?

I decide I want to open the box, but yet again, I think about it, I'm afraid to see the diaper bag contents once more. I then move the box from one side of the table to the other, like playing some sort of game with it. I look at the clock and realize that it's still 5 more hours before Jose gets home from work. Thinking it's too long of a wait, I begin to pace back and forth this time between the living room and dining area. Suddenly I stop pacing in the middle of the room. My decision is finally made! I now rapidly go straight to the box to open it.

Once opening the box, I quickly recognized the diaper. I quickly get the bag out of the box and slowly unzip it. I can now see its precious contents. The bag still has Xavier's soft little belongings. The last clothes he wore the day he died. His little favorite stuffed bunny, the bear that played his favorite lullabies, and his little music box. His soft short sleeve white t-shirt and his blue pajama pants with the little lambs jumping over clouds. His pair of blue socks and the little knitted shoes my mother-in-law made for him are all here too. I have mixed feelings and emotions about having this bag in my lap once more. I had forgotten all about it by now. The bag brings back so many memories, some good, some bad. On the one hand, seeing his clothes bring me deep sadness. And on the other hand, great happiness to be holding and smelling the baby's scents left by my baby. This bag somehow brings a little piece of my beloved son back into my arms. The scent in his little shirt makes me feel like I'm holding him again. I find sweet comfort in this. I close my eyes and I can feel him resting in my arms, and by my heart in the cold hospital room once more. Quiet tears begin to suddenly run down my cheeks. I soon get lost in the memories of before. *"Mi chiquito... Mi Amor."*

A simple thing

Like a diaper bag

Brings back both feelings of pain and joy

Simple things, such as little socks

bring back heartbreak and memories of storms

A little shirt still with his scent

Arousing my tears and regret

breaking my heart again

A simple toy like a teddy bear

Brings grief, when it should be a joy

A simple bag that was forgotten

came back to haunt my soul

I hold on to it, next to my heart

And now again in my hands, I morn

His little life that I once held

a little life with a little face I hold

this little bag now retells it all once more

That he left me so all alone

A simple thing like a diaper bag tells me so.

CHAPTER 26
MEMORIES AGAIN

My counselor says that the flashbacks will take time but eventually become less and finally disappear. "Time heals," she says. If that's true, I can't wait for that to happen. It's been a couple of days since receiving the diaper bag. For days, I sit and hold the bag in my arms at night. I sit by the window, stare at the stars, and think of Xavier. My sister has decided to keep Eddie for a longer time with her. He seems to enjoy staying with his cousins, and I need time again. The bag has made me now think about little Xavier constantly, every day and night. I have been experiencing unexpected flashbacks of the time I was with my son. His pain, the needles, the blood, the bruising, the tubes!! He appears in my dreams frequently again, holding onto my hand, crying in pain like trying to tell me something. It is real torture!

Even when I'm trying to spend time with Eddie, I can't stop thinking about Xavier. Having the diaper bag returned to me I feel, has taken me steps back instead of steps forward. This is something unexpected. Before the diaper bag was returned, I was convinced I was on my way to a slow but sure recovery. But now I'm lost.

Once more, Jose is worried about me. He understands why I opened the box and got the diaper bag on my own, and he believes that his presence in doing so would not have made a real difference in the outcome. He tells me now that it's probably something I had to, unfortunately, go through on my own. "I believe there is a reason for this diaper appearing in our lives again," he tells me. "There is a reason for everything, and this is a strong message for you. I do believe this to be true *mija*," he tells me, holding both my hands in his. "Sometimes things don't get better until they hit rock bottom." "I'm afraid that you must go somewhat alone through this journey'.

"What are you saying to me, Jose?," He quickly answers: "I believe things could only get better for you from now on." " I don't know why, but I feel something good is coming." Jose holds me in his arms, and we sit on the sofa, loving each other and thinking of what to do next. We then find ourselves staring at the diaper bag together. "Remembering when our son was alive, and this diaper bag went with us everywhere?" I can tell Jose is once more worried about me returning to my depression and what this could do to him and our little family. I can tell that by now, Jose is getting tired of holding everything together for me and our son. I know he needs an outlet or a break for his own sanity.

FLASHBACKS

The mind knows not

if it's past or present

It all feels the same

Again and again, It's all so real

Again I feel and see It all

The flash comes with no warning

Sudden frightening lightning hits

into the heart the mind and the soul

And for some reason. The mind travels back

To see and feel everything again

Not knowing or forgetting that it's only past

Because it's all so real in the now.

CHAPTER 27
THE CEMETERY

I decided to go to my daily cemetery visit and spend some time with Xavier. Since the diaper bag was returned to me, I miss him even more now, and I just can't find peace in my mind and my heart unless I feel near him. I bring with me his stuffed bunny and some fresh flowers to decorate his little tomb. Some water to cool him off from this hot sun. When I get to the foot of his tomb, I drop to my knees on the soft green grass. I begin first by praying and then greeting my baby boy, telling him I miss and love him. Then I pour water on the tombstone to clean his name and see his little face engraved in the shiny black granite.

I continue dripping the water, hoping to cool it off from the summer heat. With my hands, I begin to clean the sides of the stone by cutting and pulling out some of the long dry grass around it. With my bare hands, I cut and unknowingly dig so deep that I can feel the very moist ground underneath my fingertips. Little by little and for some reason, I feel a mad urge to keep digging deeper. I'm hoping to reach my son somehow. Again I start to dig even deeper into the soft ground.

By now, I somehow know I'm ultimately going out of my mind. All I can think about is getting my son out of his tomb. The more I dig, the more I need to hold him in my arms again. In frustration, I begin to cry like a mad woman. The desperation of not being able to reach him grows more profound and gets greater.

My crying is now out of control, and my hands are dirty and exhausted. With a few broken nails, my fingers are now numb and cramping. Desperate, I suddenly put my right cheek down on the shiny black stone, where I feel closer to him. I cry and kiss the stone as if it were his little cold stone face. The cold hard rock feels exactly as his face felt when he was in his little coffin.

That touch of cold and stone feeling has been hard ever to forget.

Soon I see a pair of soiled work boots at the foot of the tomb. I am startled at first, but I soon realize it is the Cemetery groundskeeper I've come to know in my frequent visits here. He kneels next to me to get my attention, trying to get his kind words to somehow calm me down. "*Señora, please calm down señora.*" "I'm so sorry to see you so broken like this again." "Please stop digging señora," he tells me, "don't do this to yourself." "It's a very hot day," I tell him, and my "baby must be hot and thirsty. I have to give him some water! I must hold his little hand to see how he is doing!" Once more, the groundskeeper tries to console me with his kind words reminding me that my son is in heaven now. That he now lives in a beautiful and comfortable place with God and other little angels'. He reminds me that in heaven, there is no pain, no hunger or thirst, heat or cold in heaven. "Your little son is an angel in heaven and heaven is a perfect place."

I insist by saying and repeating "My job is to take care of my baby and protect him! He needs me, I'm his mother! I can't leave him alone here anymore. I hear him cry at night for me! I can't sleep anymore." "But señora," the groundskeeper tells me, " Your son is not here in the cemetery. He is with God in heaven '' "Everyone knows that while your son was alive, you always took care of him and protected him from anything and everything. You are a great mother. Never forget that. Now calm down, I took the liberty of calling your husband, and he will be here very soon."

Suddenly I hear Jose approaching me from behind. "I knew I would come here," he said. "I'm so worried about you." He kneels on the grass to talk to me face-to-face. The groundskeeper gets up and Jose thanks him for his call and his help. "I won't be far if you need me," he tells Jose. Jose thanks him and then turns to me and asks me, "What's going on honey? What is happening to you? You were doing so well." "It's the diaper bag,'' I tell him in tears. "It brought back so many memories, so many things I thought I had forgotten! I keep seeing him dying repeatedly in my arms, I can't stand it!." "I'm sorry this is happening to you. I know his death has been tough on you. If I could take it all away from you, I would. But maybe, like I said before, getting the diaper bag back was meant to be. Sometimes to heal oneself, you must face certain things that perhaps are too painful and you rather forget. Perhaps of his little clot has been brought back to you for a real and bigger reason, revealing the purpose of his journey in this life here on earth."

"Perhaps your calling now is to close the circle? Sometimes the things like memories left behind come back to you to help you move forward."

"That doesn't make sense, I tell Jose. I don't understand what you mean or what you're saying?" "There are many things you must let go of, and somehow facing pain can heal your heart." "I learned that very same thing when I lost my brother. It wasn't until I went back to my childhood home to face some painful memories that I lived with him, that I was able to move on with my life. Some memories were happy, some sad, and some very upsetting, but all were brought back to me for a purpose. I know that now. These memories somehow brought closure to my brother's death"

I had to be brave and face those things alone because it is the way to do it. It isn't easy, but going through it you will at the end of the journey make you feel better. I strongly believe that this is what's going on with you. Some things still need to be resolved in your mourning. Time is our best friend, it was for me. Now honey, Just let time and God guide your steps. Let's go home to be with Eddie now. Remember that he is alive and at home waiting for you to play with him and hold him. Let's leave the baby his flowers and go home now. But I miss him. I miss him too, Jose tells me, but we must let him rest in peace. He is now in heaven. Remember when you told me what your grandmother always said about children that die? They go to heaven and become your guardian angel, he is your angel now, *"tu angelito de la guarda."*

This is too hard I tell him. I feel stuck and I can't move forward.." "Yes you can move forward *mija.* I will help you. My mother, your parents, and the whole family will help you through this too. Come, let's go home, your mother is bringing Eddie to us for the weekend. He wants and needs his mother more than ever. Remember he too lost a little brother, and he doesn't want to lose a mother too. He's waiting for you to take him to the park and read to him at night. I'm sure Xavier wants you to be healthy and to spend time with his brother Eddie. Can't you see that being with Eddie is like being with Xavier all at the same time? Xavier lives in Eddie and in you and everyone else in the family. His spirit has never left us. He will be with you wherever you go forever.

Come on honey let's go, Jose says as he gets up and helps me up. "But what about his tomb I ask? I have to fix it and put the soil I pulled out back in. I can't leave it like this." "I'll take care of it, don't worry, " the groundskeeper replies from afar. "Don't worry, go home as your husband says and remember what I told you. I'm sure your little angel wants you to take care of yourself and your family. Listen to what your husband says, he loves you. Soon it's all going to be better, God will give you the courage and peace you need."

I thank the groundskeeper for his kindness. Jose also thanks him. Then Jose holds my hand and we walk towards the car. I take a quick look at the tomb to see it one more time. Once in the car, Jose tells me: "I must confess to you that I'm also hurting just like you. I too went through the pain of seeing Xavier suffer so much and finally dying. I lost a part of me when he left us, but I know he is always here with me and you. I do not doubt what he says, I say to myself. 'I too feel empty and lost at times," he continues. "Sometimes I have to hold myself from falling apart like you and maybe start drinking again. But I fight it. I hold on to you, my son, and the family to be better and continue living. I believe you should try to do the same." I agree, and I tell Jose in resignation, "I will try to make things better. Thank you for your words, they make me see things differently." Jose holds my hand as we continue our drive home.

You Can't Imagine

I'm cut and I bleed so deep

But you can't see my wound

It is too deep in a dark tomb

and lives inside me

It was savagely carved into me

with the sharp knife of death

left in me for all eternity

Never to be forgotten

Never to be erased

I'm cut and I bleed, but you can't see it

Even if I dig inside me

So far into my womb and soul

I can't get it out!

And you can't even imagine it

I'm cut and I bleed

Chapter 28
Time to Go

September 14 1982

In the Bedroom with My Husband and Son

It's almost midnight, and I sit still sleepless in the corner of my bed in the bedroom where Jose and Eddie sleep. For many days now, since the cemetery visit, I've been unable to sleep a complete night's sleep. I constantly think about the empty arms Xavier left in me with. The arrival of the diaper bag has somehow taken me on a new journey, some steps back in my mourning. Jose, in his desperation, has arranged for me to go to his hometown of La Laja for some time. He, my mother-in-law, and my whole family believe this will be a good thing for my healing. I'm feeling guilty about having to leave Eddie again. But I feel I must for all our sakes. I know he will be fine with my mother and father, who greatly love him. And with my sisters, who give him so much love and attention.

A few months ago, I had two sons, today only one. I feel half alive and half dead. I need to be strong to go to this unknown place to recover from my old self. I owe this to Eddie. He needs me whole as much as I need him.

A soft ray of light slightly beams between the bedroom window shades. Through the dim light in the room, I now try to finish packing my suitcase. Trying not to wake anybody up, I slowly walk to Eddie's crib where he comfortably sleeps. There I lovingly caress his little head. I whisper I love you, telling him how sorry I am for leaving him again.

I need to be complete for you. I'll be back soon. ``Is it time?" Jose's words suddenly startled me. Is it time to take you to the airport? He says to me, still half asleep and sitting up in bed. "No, it's barely midnight," I whisper to him as I get nearer. I just can't sleep. I'm worried about leaving you and Eddie." " It's going to be alright," Jose reassures me. Eddie will be well taken care of. He is in the best place and with the right people." "The way things are right now, you're not being any good to him or yourself. Eddie sees your pain in silence and asks why you don't play with him as you used to. Does he ask why you're crying in your room so much? He is a smart little boy with instincts, and he is sensible in his feelings. This trip is not only for your health and sanity, but it will also benefit us all."

"You are visiting the people in my hometown. They are good people. My parents raised us there. I know that the family and people there will help you heal because they have come to face grave situations. Life has taught them to heal and help each other heal through tragedy. I know you'll find many things and experiences in common with them. We are all one family there, and you will be part of that too. I wish I could take this trip with you, but somebody has to pay the bills," he says to me. "You will be fine and I know you will heal," he says with confidence. "I hope so," I tell Jose, "I need to recover once more the spirit I lost in that delivery room that day." Jose gets up from bed and moves towards me to hold me in his arms. This comforts me. "I know what you went through was very difficult," he says. " I know that in my absence, you went through some very heavy things alone in the hospital. Every day I went to work thinking and worried about you and the baby being there day and night. It has been complicated for me too. Having to go to work always expecting the worst was how I spent my time. You were always with Xavier, and you gave him your all," Jose says. "You can be certain of that. I held on to Jose as tight as I could, so much so that I could feel his heart beating in my chest. I then realize that at this time, through all we've been through together, we have become one.

CHAPTER 29
THE AIRPORT "A JOURNEY BEGINS"

SEPTEMBER 14, 1982

Saying goodbye to my son and husband at the airport is hard, so after kissing them goodbye, they leave and I quickly head to the boarding area. Upon boarding the plane, I'm glad I have a window seat. Once sitting in my seat, I buckle up and try not to think about my family which I'm leaving behind. I feel somewhat excited and a bit looking forward to what Jose has told me about the village and its people. A mixture of emotions, like sadness and wonder, run through me all at the same time. And I also fear the idea of the unknown. Either way, I'm looking forward to the new journey;y and adventure and the possible healing I will receive on this trip.

Upon take off, my eyes are glued to the window. Looking at all the clouds before me. I wonder if my son and little Gabriel are amongst these clouds? This is what a part of heaven must be like. White soft clouds continuously form shapes and create a mosaic of graceful art. I feel so close to heaven up here, this must be what heaven is like.

The flight attendant suddenly startles me and asks if I want something to drink. I ask for a Coke on ice and I receive it right away. Sipping on the ice-cold coke, I wonder why this little village is called "La Laja" and what it's like. All I know about this place is that this is where Jose and his family originate for at least four generations. Jose showed me some home pictures of its beautiful countryside and green mountains. I especially like the pictures of the river and waterfalls that Jose describes as being his playground as a young boy. He tells me that the people there are simple and very loving. They are the "salt of the earth." He says these people know hardship in so many aspects. Jose is sure that my visit there will help me find me. And I wonder if I will ever find myself again. I know that getting away from L.A. doesn't mean my pain stays there. My broken heart and spirit will forever be inside with me. No matter where I go. I don't know at this time what to anticipate from this journey. I have full trust in God and my husband's love for me.

CHAPTER 30
ARRIVING IN GUADALAJARA
SEPTEMBER 14, 1982

The captain announces that we will soon land in our destination, Guadalajara. This announcement quickly brings me back from my flashback. I straighten up my seat and prepared myself for landing. Looking out the window, I can see the city, roads, and little buildings getting bigger and bigger as the plane gets closer and closer to landing. At this time, I'm looking forward to seeing my cousin Fernando who lives in Guadalajara and at times, has come to visit us in L.A. He is at the airport, ready to pick me up, as arranged on the phone with Jose, and take me to La Laja.

Having all sisters as siblings, Fernando is the closest I have to a real brother. He has always loved and respected me like an older sister. Fernando and

Jose have been good friends since the time they met. In Jose's frequent trips to La Laja to see his grandmother, Fernando has always been there for him to drive him to the countryside. Because of these visits, he has become loved and respected by the people and families there. Fernando has promised Jose that they will make sure to take me safely to La Laja. He is my connection with my childhood and my life here in this very city as a child.

The plane lands, and the unloading begins. My heart has a deep excitement and celebration for being back home, where I was born and lived until seven years old. Walking out of the plane and into the large waiting area, I quickly spot Fernando anxiously waving hello across the room. Fernando comes forward and gives me a warm embrace, which brings tears to both our eyes. "I'm so sorry for your loss and for what happened to your son," he says, and holds me tight. I can immediately feel Fernado's love for me in that embrace. These words make me feel at home right away and most of all home with my family.

Re Visiting the Old Neighborhood

The drive to La Laja begins by driving out of the airport and soon through the city of Guadalajara. The drive quickly brings back strong memories of my childhood and the family I left behind. I sit in the car not saying a word. I am now quietly enjoying the sights and smells of the city I once knew as home.

Driving through all the old familiar places and streets keeps my mind busy with vivid memories of a life I once had here. It's nice to see the old neighborhood, I tell Fernando as we drive through it. I began to recognize some familiar places, like the old **"mercado"** or market place which still stands. The faces I see in our drive through the neighborhood seem familiar even though they are complete strangers. People are walking down the sidewalks, some waiting for the bus to go to work. Women take children with their backpacks to school. Time seems to stand still here in my old neighborhood. I remember walking to school on these very streets with my little cousins like it was yesterday.

Soon we drive by my old elementary school. It's no longer whitewashed as I remember it, instead, it's now painted bright blue with white trim around the windows. The school has a playground complete with swings and a big slide. It's no longer the green clear empty area where we freely ran around playing games. We are now going to pass through what used to be our **"abuelitos"** house. This is the home where I lived with my family for the first seven years of my life.

My grandparents' corner house is now transformed into a **"tiendita"** or a neighborhood store. My heart drops a beat at the sight of the old beautiful hacienda house with its large wooden doors and windows now holding Coca-Cola, Tecate Beer, and Bimbo Bread signs on its wall. I loved this very traditional Mexican home. I find the change heartbreaking and very hard to believe. I have so many warm memories in this old place. I can still remember the smells of the wood stove cooking breakfast and my grandfather walking his horse through to the corral. I still imagine seeing my grandmother sitting outside by the front door, embroidering her kitchen towels **"servilletas"** as she greets the passersby. I see my grandfather trimming the small trees on the sidewalks. And my cousins and I, playing out in the street.

My grandfather's father bought the house after the Mexican Revolution. It was part of a large rich owner's hacienda, which was divided and purchased for very little money or in parts for a fair price to the poor working-class people. Three generations of our family lived in this home very happily. And some of my siblings, uncles, and cousins were all born in this old house. My grandfather proudly displayed many pictures of his family and his revolution comrades. Most of the photographs and relics were of the Mexican Revolution, which he was very proud of.

I remember that there was a large picture of General Franciso Villa, his revolutionary hero. The entry hall was painted bright orange and had colorful *macetas* on both sides of the *"pasillos"* or hallways. The long outside hallway led to a large kitchen. And behind the kitchen was a "corral" for my grandmother's chickens, pigs, and ducks. At times we helped feed them. And of course my grandfather's horses. What a wonderful time I had in this old house, and now sadly has become the neighborhood store. With no trace of us.

The hard times came to our family in the late 60s. Our lives suddenly began to change. Because of a national recession and lack of jobs, most of our family migrated to the United States for a chance at a better life. Eventually, each of my uncles and their families moved away, leaving my grandparents alone to care for themselves. When my grandmother mainly died of loneliness, my grandfather lost all interest in keeping up the house. When he died, the house was sold. I remember so clearly when my uncle called my father and told him so. "It's too bad we couldn't keep the house in the family," I say sadly to Fernando. "I would have loved to stay here now." "I know, but there is always my house," Fernando tells me looking back at me with a comforting smile."Mi Casa es Tu Casa" he assures me.

Our drive continues through the city's old streets and into the modern Guadalajara, complete with high-rise buildings and new streets, highways, and roads. A whole new world for me.

CHAPTER 31
THE DRIVE TO LA LAJA

SEPTEMBER 14, 1982

Fernando tells me that the drive to **La Laja** is two hours from the city. He says that he spoke with Jose's family there and they are excited to meet you finally. "They are very pleased that you'll be staying with them for a while. They are all looking forward to your visit." I feel pleased to hear those words. And I feel more relaxed about staying there. Jose tells me that the people in **La Laja** are very honest, sincere, and loving. And that I have nothing to worry about regarding being welcomed and taking very good care of there.

Before leaving the city, Fernando stops to get gasoline at a corner gas station. While waiting for the tank to fill, I noticed a young and very pregnant woman holding a young child's hand standing at her side at the bus stop. This sight quickly transports me to the time of my second pregnancy, when I was pregnant and happily holding my son Eddie by my side. I recall these carefree days of not knowing what was to come. I now know that anyone's life can change instantly and sometimes for the worse. I close my eyes and say a small prayer for them, hoping for the best for the woman and her children. I sincerely hope for the best for her and her unborn child. The tank is full, the gas attendant tells us. Fernando pays him, gets in the car, and we slowly begin driving out of the gas station. As we leave onto the side of the road, we pass by the woman standing at the bus stop with her child. Our eyes meet for a moment, and she smiles at me in recognition and a sort of gratitude, as if she knew I had just said a prayer for her and her children. I smile back and wave hello with my fingers to the little boy, and he waves back with a smile.

Soon Fernando's car begins to drive out of the city and into the beautiful green countryside. There's minimal conversation between us as of right now. It's as if they are respecting my silence. They know I'm still in mourning and need time for myself. I'm not my usual happy-go-lucky talker that they have come to know in the past. And for now, I appreciate their understanding and kindness in accepting this.

As the drive continues, I look out the window to enjoy the scenery. Both sides of the road are filled with beautiful lush plains, hills, and greenery. Driving by the sides of the hillside, I can appreciate the number of animals like cows, horses, and goats grazing in the plain's green pastures. "Is La Laja beautiful like this?" I ask Fernando. "La Laja is even more beautiful," he answers. "There are visible landmarks like waterfalls and high pine trees that make La Laja a favorite place for many to visit."

"The village is up in the mountains where the greenery is even more lush and full of nature's wonders. The people there are farmers and live off the land. So you will be able to see many fields of corn, beans and all kinds of vegetables growing. The women tend to the household chores while the children sometimes work and at times they can, play. It's almost like going back in time to a peaceful, untouched place," he continues. When visiting here I always feel welcomed and treated like I'm one of the family."

I begin to think I have nothing in common with this village or its people. I was born a city girl. I know nothing about living in the countryside. Moving from Guadalajara to Los Angeles is my experience. I am a city girl. On the other hand, Jose grew up in the countryside. I trust what he says. If he says this is the perfect place for me to begin to heal my soul and spirit, I believe him. I know that he only wants the best for me. He knows something I don't know about life and wisdom in this place. This place gave him his outlook on life. And that outlook is what I love about him. And it's the reason why I came today.

Jose grew up in this village. Like many other Mexican families, Jose's family came to the U.S. in his early teenage years. He and his family migrated to Los Angeles in search a better life and opportunities. I learned this from him when I met him. In talking and getting to know Jose, I noticed a peaceful acceptance of life and any circumstances that come his way. I must confess that I envy his calmness but this attitude of life at times drives me crazy. As a control freak, I always insist on fixing even the unfixable. On the other hand, Jose and his family tend to give no allowance to the unfixable. They have learned to move forward in any circumstance.

All in life is part of our spiritual growth, he tells me. It gives me something to think about now. I need to learn to let things pass and accept them for what they are. Jose has learned to enjoy life and all it has to offer. This is something I like about Jose and his family. They seem to have what I call the **"way"** of *La Laja.*

Because of this, I'm sure that this is what I will encounter and experience in the village on this journey. A new way to appreciate what God gives me. And recognizes that good or bad it's all for a reason. This is why Jose encouraged and convinced me to come. I know he cares about my sanity and well-being. And at the same time, the well-being of the family.

Getting closer and closer to the mountainside, I'm appreciating the scenery that is unfolding before me. I see the small water creeks streaming from the river banks and the colorful flowers adorning the roadside. The small waterfalls pour out white, almost heavenly white water. Everything else I see going up the mountainside starts giving me peace. It's almost magical and mystical. Looking out the window to witness these scenes, I briefly allow the moment to touch me. For minutes I Seem to escape my sadness. I forget my mourning and allow myself to feel alive again.

The green setting allows it for at least a few minutes. I can feel the beauty of nature and what it has to offer through every pore of my being. It feels good to open the window and feel the clean crisp and fresh air brushing against my face. The aromas of nature are also making themselves present. No one is speaking in this magical instant. Just taking it all in.

Chapter 32
Flash Back to the Beginning
September 14, 1982

In closing my eyes and enjoying the ride. I sit back in the seat to relax. By doing this I let my guard down, and somehow, without warning or wanting it, my mind takes me to an event in the past.

"You're about two months pregnant," I hear the unexpected news from my OBGYN. Hearing the doctor say these words. I could only think about my still very young son Eddie, who is only 16 months old. "Congratulations Mrs. Lopez, your second baby will be here in seven months."

The doctor's words echo over and over in my head. I wonder what Jose's reaction to the quick addition to the family will be. At this time I don't know what to think or say to the doctor. I stay silent. This is all so unexpected. " It's not that I don't want more children," I tell the doctor, "it's just that I didn't expect it to be this soon." "This surprise happens more than you think, to a lot of young mothers just like you." "But look at the bright side," the doctor continues, "your children will play and grow up together." "Congratulations again, and I will see you next month, '' he tells me as he walks out of the examining room.

Leaving the examination room, I'm not sure why I feel so saddened by the news. I just don't know why I feel this way. Somehow my heart tells me something about this pregnancy is going to change my life forever.

"That's wonderful news!" Jose says when I get home and tell him the news. "Another baby!" "Eddie is going to have a little companion to play with." These words made me very happy, but behind my mind, not know why I still feel sad. The whole family rejoiced at the news and had many plans for a soon-to-be baby shower. I soon told Eddie about the news and he too was excited about having a little brother or sister to play with soon. Everyone is excited about the news. I'm still feeling like something bad is coming my way. My motherly instinct somehow warned me of something.

CHAPTER 32
ARRIVING IN LA LAJA
SEPTEMBER 14, 1982

As Fernando announces to me that we are getting closer to the village. His words quickly bring me back from my flashback to the present. I'm getting nervous now, thinking about meeting everyone in La Laja. I suddenly begin to feel butterflies in my stomach. This is it! It's time! I think to myself as I take a deep breath. "Don't worry about anything," Fernando tells me, "I have been coming to visit here many times before, and I always feel so welcomed." Fernando was introduced to La Laja by Jose on one of his visits back home. He has always been the ride from the city to the mountains of La Laja for Jose and now for me. Fernando is no stranger to this place; I understand he is very well-loved and respected there.

From a good distance, I can now see a small blanket of small whitewashed houses with terracotta rooftops in the middle of the mountains. "That is La Laja," Fernando points out. We are getting closer to the village. Then, I suddenly noticed something interesting on the right of the dirt road. I quickly ask Fernando what this place is. He explains that it was a cemetery. Fernando stops at the side of the road to explain that this is the local cemetery. When looking closer from the car, I notice that this cemetery has many colorful tombstones resembling little traditional churches and bell towers instead of the rigid rows of black, shiny granite. The tombs are all very colorful. They are painted with different bright colors and are in different lengths, shapes, and sizes. They are all different, nicely, and carefully adorned with different colored paper and plastic flowers. Some tombs have pictures of their loved ones. The atmosphere in this cemetery, although sad in origin, seems festive.

The spirit of death is present, but clearly, as a part of life. It's like a sort of continuum or communion with life.

Contrary to the dark stone frames that adorn the Los Angeles cemetery. The black granite stones are a constant reminder of death and separation and the ongoing sadness that occurs at the end of life. Looking at this place, I realize that this is a possible reason for my coming to the village. I had to see this place, where there is a different way of looking at and experiencing the death of a loved one. I thank Fernando for stopping here.

We now leave the cemetery to continue our drive toward the village. I can now see the town's small church bell tower gleaming in midday sunlight. When finally entering the village, I can see a simple line of white "pueblo" houses on dirt streets. There is a small, simple town plaza in what seems to be the town center, with some small trees and white metal benches. The glare of the sunlight is gleaming between the trees' leaves, making it hard to see their fruits. The plaza is decorated with lines of colorful red, white, and green paper **(papel picado).** Decorations in the plaza are an old festive tradition, Fernando tells me as he points them out to me. "The town just celebrated their patron saint yesterday." And tomorrow is the Mexican Independence from Spain celebration, which will also be celebrated in the plaza.

I see a small church that is also colorfully decorated. "This is why the plaza is so beautifully decorated today," he continues. Even knowing that the decorations were for the patron saint. Going by the plaza made us feel that this decorative welcome is also for us.

Continuing to head down to what seems to be the village's main street, I can see a small hill at a short distance. I now guess from Jose's description that this is where his family lives. I can now see the people happily waving and waiting for the visitors to arrive finally. Once at the top, the car stops, and we begin slowly getting out of the car to be greeted by the whole family.

The warm welcome makes me feel special. I can't believe such warm and friendly manners in greetings still exist. I can tell that the whole family is present. Men, women, and children. From the eldest to the youngest person in the compound, they surround me with a smile. I am first introduced to the elders and patriarchs of the family, Tia Maria and Tio Juan. They are two of the five remaining founders of the village and are well respected by the people of La Laja.

CHAPTER 33
MEETING EVERYONE

On arrival, and once getting out of the car, Tia Maria and Tio Juan begin the introductions of the family. First, I met the women and the children of the compound. These are simple women with beautiful faces and long braided hair. They wear clean clothes and beautiful embroidered aprons. The women are dressed in what is their Sunday best. The children are also dressed in clean white garments and well-combed hair.

There seems to be a lot of preparation for this beautiful and simple welcome. The third and final group I meet is the men in the compound. These men seem to be hard-working men, looking very rugged and strong. Their hands are calloused and scarred from years of hard labor and farming. Although somewhat quiet and very respectful, they too, seem to be happy with the visitors. The whole family group is composed of, first, second, third, and fourth-generation cousins, aunts, and uncles. No distinctions are made among the family members. They are brothers among them.

"We were hoping my sister Domitila, your mother inlaw would accompany you on this journey," Tio Juan said. " We miss her and her family very much. Their visits here are not very frequent, we wish they were closer. I tell them she misses La Laja too and that she told me all about her life here and her family. And that she will try her best to be here soon.

A shower of warm hugs and welcoming gestures continued invading my cousin Fernando and me. It's been a long time since I felt this kind of welcome. In receiving so much of this attention and love, I have momentarily forgotten my own family for a minute.

My eyes wander around the beautiful modest and clean stone patio. The patio is surrounded by colorful *macetas* with beautiful plants and flowers. On the right side of the patio is a kitchen composed of a clay oven, a large comal, and a wood-burning stove. There are colorful plates and cups or "*Jarros*" hanging in a circular formation decorating the clay kitchen wall. A loaf of masa sits in a big clay bowl, ready to be used. Another clay pot is boiling beans or *frijoles* in the wood stove.

When the introductions are made, the family group walks and leads us toward the center of the patio, where a large wooden handmade family table and chairs await us. The table is carefully adorned with baskets of colorful fruit sitting in each corner of the large table. The table is also adorned with beautiful wildflower arrangements and hand-embroidered *manteles* or tablecloths. I am so impressed by the simple beauty of this place. The elders take their seats at the head of the table and the guests are asked to sit beside them. The children giggle and stare at the new guest as they tell secrets to each other. Everyone here seems to have a role or job to follow.

Two of the six women begin to make tortillas with their plain hands. *(Torteando)* Another two walk over to stir the food in the pots, which allows the flavors and aromas to escape into the kitchen and out to the patio.

CHAPTER 34
THE FOOD

SEPTEMBER 14, 1982

Two women soon begin to serve food on large clay plates. The menu includes Chiles *rellenos, arroz, red mole, guacamole, sopes,* and ***tostadas*** are all part of the menu and all in celebration of having us as a guest. I am overtaken by the wide variety of so much delicious Mexican food. The smells, textures, and flavors are incomparable to anything else I've had in the past. I could tell the women worked so hard on this welcoming traditional banquet. They want to make sure to serve the best Mexican **"antojitos."**

The women serving the food frequently ask if we like or are enjoying the food. I understand that asking these kinds of questions is common and very important to women cooking and preparing food. The women here are very much encouraged by the positive acknowledgments made to them by visitors, especially when it comes to their cooking. The women want to make sure to please both the palate and the heart. They want to make sure that their guests are both delighted and satisfied with what they cook and serve at the table.

The food is delicious, and the conversation is lively, especially between Fernando and the men. At almost the end of the meal, and all the serving is done, the women finally join the table to eat. A joke pops out in the middle of the conversation, and the whole table, children included, laughed and enjoyed it. I can already see that the people here are kind and very hospitable. So far Jose is right about the warm spirit of these people. Once everyone is settled at the table, I see the young children eating in their mother's lap, and I remember my son Eddie. He, too, likes to sit in my lap to eat his meal or share mine. I begin to miss my little family. Except for my cousin, everyone at this table is new to me.

The dinner ended, and the end of the day had come. The evening is near and after a few hours of talking, eating, and enjoying, Fernando announces his return to Guadalajara. The family is ready to say goodbye to him now. With a strong embrace, I say goodbye to my cousin and tell him to return soon. Fernando reminds me that I will be alright here and that he is just a phone call away. Everyone says goodbye and wishes him a safe ride home. One of the women hands Fernando some homemade tortillas wrapped in a beautifully embroidered napkin, **"servilleta,"** to take home to his wife Laura and ask him to bring her next time. He agrees.

The men shake Fernando's hand, and we all accompany him to their car. You are in good hands, Fernando tells me with a smile. "Come back soon," the family says as he gets in the car. Fernando's car is turned on and slowly moving down the hill. By now, all hands are still waving goodbye until, eventually, the car passes through the plaza and begins to fade off to the main road that heads back to the city.

CHAPTER 35
MY FIRST NIGHT IN LA LAJA
SEPTEMBER 14, 1982

It's time to retire to our beds and sleep. Tia Maria tells me, you will be sleeping there, she points to Rafaela's house. I say good night to everyone left in the kitchen. I'm then led to Rafaela's house, where she explains I will be sleeping. From the patio, we walk into a large long room with plastic chairs and many pictures on the wall. I'm taken to the corner of the long room, where there is a small wooden bed against the back wall. I see that my luggage is already there in the corner of the improvised room. The bed area is separated from the rest of the room with a simple plastic curtain that makes the sleeping area somewhat private.

The bed has beautifully colorful embroidered pillowcases and a white knitted bedspread. There is a small window at the very top of the wall, where I can see the moonlight. A small wooden handmade table sits at the side of the bed, holding a tin can with some very aromatic and colorful flowers. This is your bed, Rafaela says softly. I will bring you a blanket. Gracias, I tell her, you're very kind. I hope you're comfortable here. This is your home for the time you are here with us. This is the house where your husband Jose was born and spent most of his childhood. She says to me again in her soft voice.

The little corner room is warm and inviting like the rest of the room. It has a warm and inviting family feeling. One feels this warmth upon entering the room right away. This was the first house built in the compound. I understand all four generations have come to live here at one time or another. It is evident that this house has seen many generations come and go. The testaments are posted in black and white pictures randomly placed on the wall. An old black-and-white blurry photo of the first settlers is in the center of the wall. The men are posing in two straight lines, one standing and the other sitting. Both lines of men are dressed in white cloth or "manta" proudly holding the rifles they used to protect the village and their families from the enemy. The men also wear bullet belts making an x across their chests. Some are wearing the typical large peasant revolutionary hats.

Next is a picture of the Blessed Mother (Guadalupe) and a crucifix at her side. The rest of the wall has pictures that show generations of grandparents, weddings, and grandchildren. Some calendars from local town stores make part of the wall decor. The more I see my little corner in the room, the more I fall in love. It feels warm and welcomed here.

The Outhouse

I ask Rafaela about going to the bathroom and taking a shower before going to bed. She tells me that most people here bathe in the morning by heating water on a wooden fire. Or wait for the afternoon and bathe in a small creek under the sun. I had not considered the bathroom situation, and Jose never told me that something like this would happen. I tell her I have no choice but to wait and bathe in the morning with warm heated water.

But using the toilet is another matter and a real adventure here. I soon discover that the bathroom is outside, away from the house, an *"out house."* I have to leave the house to use the " toilet'' I ask Rafaela with great concern. Yes, she answers me. The outhouse is used by all of us, including children, at all times and in all kinds of weather. I am now told that there is no other place in the darkness or rain. I now begin to think, "What have I gotten myself into ''? I have to go to the bathroom before I go to bed, so I have no other choice but to go there now

Rafaela asks Regina to accompany us to the outhouse. They use an oil lamp to light up the small dirt trail that leads us to the outhouse. On the way there, I can hear the creatures of the night, crickets and frogs, etc., which seem to be somewhere very near me. All this brings chills to my spine. It makes me want to hurry to the outhouse as quickly as possible, do my thing quickly, and return to the house. On entering the outhouse, I find it in complete darkness. I can soon smell a foul odor coming from what seems through shadows to be a hole covered by an old wooden seat. This is the toilet, Regina points out to me as she brings the lamp in. I begin to feel a sort of nausea suddenly coming over me. It's hard to breathe

Regina finds this to be funny and begins to laugh. Rafaela signals her to stop laughing and both hand me the lamp and some privacy. I slowly start to try and sit on the wooden seat, which seems old and possibly full of splinters. Trying to hold my breath, I carefully try to sit, afraid of what may crawl up my legs around me. As I carefully sit, I lift my feet off the ground, making using the toilet even more uncomfortable.

In trying to hurry, I look around and notice a small roll of toilet paper on the side of the floor. I quickly grab it, terrified that something might be hiding in the center of the roll. I decide to risk it, and I use it. I then hurry, put my pants up, and get out as quickly as possible. The two women are outside waiting for me. Reaching for the old wooden door, almost dark by now, I reach for the wooden knob to open the old door I come to feel something gooey and slimy moving in my hand. I scream in a panic. The two women quickly open the door and help me out. Looking at my hand, we discover that I have almost come to squish a small frog hiding in the old door knob. I quickly shake my hand in panic. I step out the door and promptly catch my breath. I drastically rub my hands on some tree leaves that Rafaela hands me. Regina tries to hold back her laughter. As she covers her mouth, I can see her eyes bulging trying not to laugh. By now, I'm using the oil lamp all on my own. I quickly move forward and lead the women back to the main house. I stop for no sound this time, I just want to get back to the place where I feel it's safe from any sort of creature.

Once back in the house, I quickly ran to find refuge in my little corner space. I then quickly get into my small bed. I asked Rafaela if any creatures come into the house at night. She assures me that critters don't usually come in. I took that answer as a NO, just so I could sleep. Rafaela and Regina finally say goodnight, and soon the lights go off in the large room.

The room is dark and silent, with only the sounds heard of crickets and a few dogs barking in the distance. The only light coming into the room is from the corner window, where a full moon shines. I've now been left alone with my thoughts and fears. I soon find myself desperately trying to fight some sad memories that, by now once more, are sharply floating in my mind.

I quickly wrap myself tightly into the blankets to prevent any animal from crawling or entering my personal space. I lay there praying and trying to search for pleasant thoughts and memories. But I'm feeling all alone, so far away, and scared. It is almost impossible for me to think good thoughts. After what seemed like a few hours of restless turning in bed, I somehow fell asleep, and my dreaming took me back to another haunting flashback. This time in a new nightmare form:

I'm arriving for my third visit to my OBGYN's office. Again, the heart monitor is out of service, it's now floating in the air on top of me in the examining room, and the nurse sings: "Lalala monitor is not working again La Lala." The doctor comes in wearing a crazy-looking green party hat and red party glasses. He is not surprised by this broken monitor at all. "I don't think this is a bad thing at all, Mrs. Lopez," and laughs! Hahahah. He laughs so loud that my ears can't stand it, hahaha. I can't hear my baby's heartbeat! I scream over and over, but no one listens. I quickly leave the examining room and walk into a dark and dingy hallway surrounded by purple lights and a broken-down examining bed. "Lie down in this bed," The nurse tells me, and I run as fast as I can out of that room. Now I'm in another long dark hallway where I begin to see in between dim yellow lights and a thin wall of smoke that both sides of the walls are used as some sort of egg incubators for sad and broken pregnant women. The rows are filled with pregnant women, who all sit with their heads bowed, not saying a word. Just waiting for their eggs to hatch. I see them close. I see their faces. They all look like me! Something is wrong! My heart beats faster. I say something! But no one listens. A clown now appears at the end of the hall and says, "Don't worry...Be happy." I scream: Please get another monitor! Please, doctor, I beg you! I want to listen to my son's heart! Dr. Ross and the nurses laugh, dance in circles, and tell me "Nothing is wrong," "Everything is just my imagination."

I am somehow shaken out of this terrible nightmare. I find myself now sweating and shaking, and sitting in a little bed in the middle of the night. The dream is too real to me. The fear of not doing enough for my child eats at my soul and my conscience. I now try to keep from crying, but it's impossible. I begin to cry as low and quietly as possible, trying not to wake anybody in the room on the other side of the curtain. It was not my imagination! My baby was sick! I try to console myself and look out the window and see the moon beaming in the small corner of the room. How am I going to survive my time here? I ask myself. It's day one and this nightmare has already made me feel like running and returning home tomorrow.

Doubts are coming quickly into my mind. I feel I have nothing in common with anyone here. That no one will understand. How am I going to survive this? I don't know how this place or these people will be able to help me when I can't get things out of my mind. Now I wonder with much doubt, why did I accept to come here? My remorse eats me alive in thinking I should have gone to see another OB-GYN or doctor or just fought Doctor Ross' opinion on the monitor. My guilt is so heavy.

CHAPTER 36
MEETING THE WOMEN

My first night in La Laja was long. I woke up in the morning still shaken from the awful nightmare. I was awakened by multiple animal sounds coming through the small window. Chickens, cows, and goats all say good morning simultaneously. I can also hear the sounds of women talking and cooking in the kitchen. Children running around, and the voices of some men leaving to work in the fields. I quickly get up and get dressed and walk out the door. I notice everybody has begun their day by now. I walk to the *outhouse*, which looks even more frightening in the daytime and feels and smells the same. I quickly come out of the outhouse and wash my face and hands and brush my teeth in a "**pila**" or tub of water by the outhouse. I then walk over to the kitchen. The women and children greet me as I enter the kitchen area. **"Buenos dias"** they say very kindly. I then answer *buenos dias* and I am soon directed to sit at the table for breakfast.

Tia Maria and Tio Juan are already sitting at the table. Did you sleep well? Tio Juan asks me. I tried, I told him. But I miss home. You will be feeling at home here in a few days, he says with a smile. Looking around the kitchen, I'm overtaken by everything that was going on. Women are cooking, some are cleaning and some making tortillas. Everything smells so good, the eggs and beans are being fried, and the quesadillas made with homemade cheese are almost ready in the comal. A bowl of freshly made salsa is sitting in the middle of the table. How can I say no to all this? It smells so good, and everything looks delicious. After the delicious traditional **"rancho"** breakfast, Tio Juan explained to me that today is September 15 and tomorrow 16 is the Mexican Independence Celebration and that later on there was going to be a celebration in the plaza. He now says that he and the rest of the men go to their daily labors till noon so they can attend the festivities. Everyone seems to be very excited and looking forward to this celebration. I am not excited at all.

Tia Maria then says: "Since yesterday there was no real time to meet the women on an individual basis, I will take this time to introduce each one to you.." She begins by introducing me to her oldest son Manuel's wife **Rafaela.** A woman was brought to the family from another compound in the village. Rafaela is well known for her calm spirit and good cooking. Both Regina and Socorro are good cooks, but no one cooks like Rafaela, for she's the keeper of old traditional family recipes left behind by generations. Rafaela has four children, two boys, and two girls. The boys are sent to farm the land with their father, and the girls learn the household chores. That's what all children here do. And that is what Rafaela and Manuel and the generations before them also did as children. Rafaela is a quiet soul with nothing much to say. She has a warm look on her face and a soft voice to go with it.

Socorro is married to Marcos, the second son of Tioon Juan and Dona Maria. Socorro is one of the youngest wives here in the compound. Marcos and Socorro have three small children. She is also brought from another compound. The same place where Rafaela is from. Rafaela and Socorro are first cousins. Socorro is the total opposite of Rafaela. She is not quiet but very witty and is always finding. She has a loud voice and is not bashful with comments. Socorro's specialty is healing and knowledge of herbs. She learned this from her grandmother who taught her the trade of "curandera." Socorro, like her grandmother, is known as the village *"Yerbera"* or herb healer **"Curandera."** Since her early teens, Socorro has been helping people with their illnesses along with her mother. People trust them and believe in their knowledge of healing herbs and ointments.

Regina is another young girl, almost the age of Socorro. She is married to Antonio, the third son, who is Regina's fourth cousin. Regina likes to sew. She hopes to have her sewing machine someday, but at the moment, she uses her sister's pedal sewing machine to sew everything by hand. She has two little girls who she sews dresses for whenever a small piece of cloth or an old dress is thrown out and available. Regina is very creative. She designs and hand-stitches beautiful shirts and blouses. Both Socorro and Regina have a good sense of humor. Because of their spontaneous wit and thinking, they tend to pick up people's spirits whenever they're around. Regina likes to sing when she cleans and washes the kitchen floor and patio. She leaves them so clean and smelling like fresh flowers. Another love for Regina is tending to the gardens and machetes. Regina talks and sings to the plants and she says that they respond to her with their beauty.

Marina is a timid woman but a very strong woman who mostly keeps to herself. She is married to Alfonso,

Don Juan's nephew, and they have been married for over fifteen years. Marina grew up in the village, and she and Alfonso have known each other since childhood. Marina at times struggles with depression, followed by the tragic loss of her two young children who drowned in the river. Marina is the midwife of the village. She has learned the trade from her mother and grandmother. Marina is well respected among the women of the village. She also helps the women heal **"Cuarentena"** after deliveries. For the 40 days, she offers these mothers nutrition and herbs to fully have them come to a full recovery. Marina, too has a tender loving spirit. Her happy approach to life quickly changed and was tinted after the tragedy with her children. Alfonso's reaction to the tragedy is that of blaming his wife. They have grown distant from each other in their marriage. Marina is quiet and kind but keeps mostly to herself. It is tough to be approached by a stranger like me.

Elena, on the other hand, is very friendly and very approachable. She is the youngest child of Tio Juan and Tis Maria's children. She is seventeen and expected to be married soon to her fiance, who has gone to El Norte to make some money and come and marry her. Although Santiago has been gone for over two years, Elana believes he will return soon to marry her. Elena's job in the family comes naturally to her. She is to watch over the small children when their mothers tend to their chores. They are mostly her little cousins or nephews and nieces. Her Love for children is evident. You can see it when she plays with them and teaches them letters and sounds. She tells me that she dreams of one day being a real teacher. And at times she creates a little school or classroom on the patio. She also teaches the children songs and how to write their names on paper. The mothers appreciate this because they can do their chores and know their children are well cared for. Elena dreams of one day becoming a real teacher and, once married, having her children.

The women I meet are all warm and welcoming. Slowly I began to feel welcome and accepted here by each of them. I Don't quite feel like a stranger right now. Now that I know a little bit about women and their families, I feel more comfortable around them.

"Now let's all get ready for the fiesta in the plaza," Elena comes to the kitchen announcing to the group. First, all the children and their mothers go and bathe in the river." The mothers then go to tend to their children. Rafaela and Tia Maria stay with me and heat some water for me to have what they call a "bucket bath" *"baño de jicara."* This bucket bath is all new to me. I was unsure where or how to start, but they soon showed me how it was done.

After my bath, I got dressed and waited on the patio as I was told for everyone, including the children, to don and be ready to go to the plaza. Little by little, the children begin to appear on the patio, with their clothes nicely neat and ironed. White shirts with red or green bows symbolize the flag colors. Although I could tell their clothes were not new, they were nicely kept for special occasions like this. The boys had their hair combed back, and the girls wore their hair in braids complete with beautiful red, white, and green ribbons. The women soon appear one at a time, wearing their Sunday best with their green and red *rebozos* ready to go celebrate. Tia Maria hands me a red *rebozo,* to wear and not feel left out. Although I was in no condition or mood to celebrate anything that night, I decided to go with the family to the plaza for a little while.

CHAPTER 37
16 OF SEPTEMBER CELEBRATION
SEPTEMBER 15-16, 1982

The town plaza looks beautifully decorated with Mexican flags, ribbons, flowers, and green, red, and white paper decorations. The ambiance in the plaza is a happy one. There is music playing, people walking and saying hello to each other. I also see some men on horses. The little food stands around the little plaza selling everything from *tacos, elotes, aguas frescas, churros,* and so on, caught my attention. I remember this from my childhood visits to the plaza in Guadalajara. Soon after arriving in the plaza, the children take off and run around with their little cousins and friends. Everyone greets each other with glee and smiles at me as if they know about me.

We finally found an empty bench to sit on. Rafaela. Tia Maria, Socorro, and I sit and wait for the town mayor to come out and make his speech. The Mayor's speech is about commemorating this special day in Mexican history. Mexican Independence. Elena is in charge of the children who will make the presentation of the National Flag and the Flag Salute. I have never seen so much pride in a flag and a national festivity like this. The event was very well organized and everyone, including the bystanders, knew exactly what to do.

After a few minutes of waiting, the town mayor appears dressed in a worn-out black suit with a green, white, and red banner across his chest. The children follow behind him with the flag. Everyone is ready to begin the ceremony once all participants are on top of the patriotic adorned kiosk. First, the mayor welcomes everyone in the plaza and leads the children in the flag salute.

Tio Juan comes to sit with me and the other women on the bench, and begins to explain the importance of this historical event and celebration to me. He says: "The mayor will be reading to the people the traditional speech of *"El Grito de Dolores."* "This speech was the one originally given by a priest named *Padre Miguel Hidalgo* y *Costilla*, who rang his church bell at midnight on September 15, 1810, declaring war on Spain. It happened in the town of Dolores. Father Hidalgo along with other rebel leaders, led a massive rebellion against the Spaniards and eventually won a triumphant war against Spain." And now he says: "The church bells will ring, symbolizing what occurred that night of rebellion."

Once the mayor's speech is over the church bells begin to ring. Soon everyone begins to chant "Viva Mexico!" The mariachi begins to play "El Son de La Negra," and everyone celebrates by throwing red, green, and white confetti up in the air! "It is a proud moment for us Mexicans," Tio Juan says. "This date 16 of September and its heroes, and their bravery, also helped us fight the Mexican Revolution in their memory exactly one hundred years later in 1910."

In my years living in the United States, I had forgotten this celebration and its importance to the Mexican people. I remember this celebration as a child when everyone in our family went to the main plaza in Guadalajara and participated in celebrations like these. I was a child when I first witnessed this, it never touched me as it has today with intense patriotic measures. I am a Mexican and will always be, no matter where I live, and sitting in this plaza tonight makes me feel very proud of my roots. "Viva Mexico!" Everyone chanted and for a few hours, I was in a whole new, yet familiar world of my past. For a few hours, I was free from my mourning and enjoying the moment. I wrapped myself and held on to my green white and red rebozo with pride.

Chapter 38
The Founding Of La Laja

SEPTEMBER 22, 1982

After the celebrations of the 16 of September event, I had some questions regarding the founding of La Laja. I wasn't quite sure how it tied to the Mexican Revolution, as Jose told me. So today, after breakfast, Tia Maria promised to take me aside to a corner of the patio and tell me the story of the origins of La Laja.

She first begins by telling me that: "During the Revolution, these high Sierra mountains, where La Laja sits, were carefully and strategically chosen by three main families for protection. She explains that during 1910-1920 the Mexican Revolution changed many lives in Mexico. Many people were persecuted for rebelling against the landlords and the government during this time. The rebellion of the poor farmers and peasants like us, who were tired of the injustices that the land owners had on us, had grown, and it became dangerous to live in towns and especially in the cities."

"My grandparents were farmers who rebelled against all these injustices" Tia Maria explains, "and as a result of this rebellion, many of our people were persecuted and mercilessly killed. Some others were chased out of their lands. As a small child, I saw whole families perish and or be separated. Women were raped, by vicious soldiers and bandits. Some male children were taken to serve as servants or soldiers."

"This was a horrific time to live in Mexico, " she says with tears in her eyes,," especially for the poor." She puts her hands on the side of her face to wipe her tears. "My grandfather described the scene as hell *"el infierno."* Soon says Tia Maria says: " can't forget or take those memories lightly" and begins to sob.

People like my family ran from attacks and were forced to leave their homes and everything else behind. "It was so terrible," she says: "The people in their desperation searched for refuge wherever they could find safety. In the northern parts of the state of Jalisco, the high mountains or the Sierra became prime places for our people to hide. My grandfather told me that the Sierra offered high mountains and much greenery or foliage enough to hide from the soldiers. But on the other hand, there were other dangers. Starting with dangerous animals like bobcats that lived wildly up here. Many types of snakes include rattlesnakes, insects, and venous spiders. The risk of being bitten or attacked by these animals was seen as a lesser risk than staying below to fight a war.

" I remember hearing the men," she continues to tell me, "talking about a great Revolutionary leader in the south named Emiliano Zapata and in the north Francisco Villa. These two leaders gave hope to the peasants to one day get justice. **"It is better to die standing than live on our knees."** was Emiliano Zapatas' main message for the people, and is what kept them going. My people believed in General Zapata's words because he lived and knew well of the injustices.."

Tia Maria tells me sadly, "my family and other families exposed themselves to great dangers by escaping to the Sierra mountains for shelter. The high mountains and hillsides help prevent sudden soldier attacks, but the cold weather, which at times was freezing, took another toll on older adults and at times on us young children. I was lucky to have survived," she says.

"The lack of food made it hard for mothers to feed their children. We the children, all suffered from malnutrition. In these mountains, I lost many loved ones from starvation and illness. At times the only food available for us were wild roots and cacti or *NOPALES*. With some luck, men hunted for rabbits, wild boar, and some deer at certain times of the year. I don't remember ever having a full stomach as a child during this time.

"As the revolution continued for a few more years, the bloodshed left many widows, orphans, and incomplete families to tend to themselves. I was left without a mother or grandmother at age 7. It then inevitably became my duty to tend to my father, grandfather, and four younger siblings. I never had a childhood and I married at 14. Taking care of people is what I've known to do and have done all my life."

"Like many villages in Mexico during this time, Tia Maria continues, La Laja began with four surviving families. My grandparents and three other families formed a small resistance group set up in these hills. They survived all the horror of the revolution and eventually formed what is known today as La Laja."

"One of the original people who survived were my father and Tio Juan's parents. The surviving people passed on the tradition of gratefulness and always thanked God for our home, family, and survival. They taught us never to forget the struggles of our families in the past. That our only true refuge is God. No matter how poor the people are here, Tia Maria says, We are always happy and grateful to have some food on our tables and a decent roof over our heads and, most of all, our families. The Revolution made us humble people, and we all realize that for us what really matters in life is love, family, and most of all survival."

What a story, I say to myself quietly as I thank Tia Maria for sharing this with me. Now many things make more sense to me in regards to Jose and his family values. The whole experience of **"surviving"** made Jose and his family grateful for having each other. Family, health, shelter, and food are all that matter. This is the spirit of the people in this place, and places like this with similar hardships. I'm beginning to feel lucky to be in a place like this and to learn about life from these simple people with a whole new perspective.

Tia Maria's story touches me. It makes me think about my values in life, most importantly when it comes to love and family. I now realize God has been good to me and my family back home. We have been fortunate in not seeing or living the horrors of war. Tia Maria ends her story by telling me that "life is good now" and God is good to us.

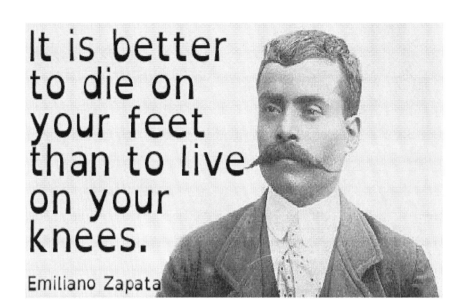

It is better to die on your feet than to live on your knees.

Emiliano Zapata

CHAPTER 39
THE DROWNINGS
OCTOBER 1, 1982

By now I have somewhat come to feel more comfortable with myself and more at home with the families here in the compound. Although it is still very difficult to be away from home, it has become a bit more bearable for me. The women include me in their chores, customs, and conversations, making me more comfortable around them.

Today, after breakfast and after all the chores are done, Regina and Socorro invite me for a walk along the river bank. They begin by showing me the small beautiful waterfalls on the hillsides. The site gives me so much peace to see. They tell me that these are the places where they come to bathe at certain times of the year. As we walk further in, Regina points to the deep side of the river, to what seems to be a very rebellious part. They then decide to share an unfortunate story about Marin's children. One that took place on this very side of the river. They begin to tell me that this place is the very place where their two nephews drowned. These children were Marina's children, they say and pause. With much respect and some curiosity, I began to ask them for details on what happened.

Regina begins the story with discretion in her tone of voice: "Eight years ago, on a Monday just like today, on our usual laundry day, the women of the compound gathered their clothes and sheets that needed to be washed and headed to the river as always. This was a normal chore for us. We all went to the river to do our weekly laundry. Marina and other women took their smaller children with them instead of leaving them alone at home. Marina took her two youngest children with her while her older ones worked with their father in the fields. Elena, the youngest of the women and closest in age to her little cousins, came along to help watch over the children. Usually, when the women washed, all mothers would help keep a short eye on each other's children. On this particular day, Marina leaves her young four-year-old in charge of watching her one-year-old brother. Something she had done before, as other women did too. It is an understanding that the older children watch the youngest to help their mothers.

When Marina and the women began to do their washing and tell stories of what is going on in the village or the aches and pains of their husbands, they noticed that the river was quickly rising and that the current was too rampant and very dangerous for a day like this. Like the others, Marina continued washing and continuously often looked back to check on her two young children. She sees her four-year-old daughter playing in the sand with her cousins and Elena in the sand. Then looks at her baby, who seems to be fast asleep. Marina, seeing her children safe, continues her wash. After rinsing some clothes, she gets off her knees and walks over to the rocks to lay the wet clothes on to dry. She quickly gets caught up in finding bigger rocks for her clothes to dry quicker and loses sight of her children for just seconds. "Seconds later," Regina continues the story, "we see a terrible site in front of our eyes. I began to scream and call Marina when I saw her toddler in the water. When Marina looked toward us, she saw that we were trying to save her young son from the fierce and deadly current. Before Marina can react, in seconds, her four-year-old daughter runs and jumps into the water, trying to save her little brother. By now, Marina has jumped in, and Socorro and I follow. All women are, by now, trying to save the children. At this, we are all trying to fight the strong current to at least save the four-year-old daughter, who is effortlessly trying to reach her little brother, whom the river has already taken. Socorro and I did all we could to save the little girl, but she was rapidly pulled away from safety by the spreading current and, like her brother, quickly disappeared in the violent current. In a great panic, Marina screams at the top of her lungs for her children! By now, we are all trying to save Marina from being carried away like her children. Marina desperately tries to pull herself away from us. She desperately begs us to let her go! That she wants to go with her children! But we knew that letting her go would lead to her inevitable drowning and death. *"Let me go," she screamed! "I want to die too"* Socorro and I held on to Marina as much as we could as we painfully witnessed the horrific disappearance of Marina's two children. The current was fast and quickly passed on, taking all things in sight. Not being able to do anything else, the women cry and hold on to each other. The devastation is too much for Marina, and she faints. Rafaela and Elena help take the unconscious Marina out of the water. The children huddled together, scared and crying at the terrible sight. Somehow the men got the news and were at the river site within minutes. The whaling and painful cries by the men, women, and children were unbearable and heard by the whole village.

One day after the incident the children were found at the end of the river bed. Their bodies were covered in mud, wrapped, and tangled in dry branches and vines. Rafaela and Elena cleaned the bodies and wrapped them in white sheets and placed their little bodies in two wooden coffins made by their grandfather. Even though Marina wanted to see her children, the elders of the family protected her by not allowing her to see them in their physical condition the children were found in.

The two coffins were placed in the center of the Patio. Soon the whole patio was filled with flowers and people on their knees praying the rosary. Mariana sat by the two coffins in a state of deep and unbearable sadness. The women sit around her and constantly reminded her that she still has to live for her other four children. Marina sobbed with a great sense of guilt and anguish. She cried and said over and over that it was all her fault. Her grief was so great that it touched everyone on the patio and the village. Mariana's husband, Alfonso, got drunk and was very much in pain. He sat outside the patio with the men. Some men sat with him, trying to console him. "Only time can heal with bottles of tequila," they told him. Tia Maria told Marina as she lovingly caressed her face, "All things will pass." " God only knows the reason for this tragedy, and one must learn to accept it." Marina sat quietly and listened to Tia Maria's words without any response. These words meant nothing to her at the moment. "I understand that," I tell them.

Little by little, as time went by, Mariana slowly began to recover. Unable to forget her little ones, she keeps herself going as much as she can. Everyone agrees that Marina is not the woman she use to be before the drowning. Something inside her died in the river that day. Despite this devastating situation in her life, Marina's faith in the Blessed Mother de *"Guadalupe" is very strong and growing every day. This helps* her accept her tragic situation. She knows that the Blessed Mother also violently lost her son, and therefore she identifies with her fate. The guilt of not having watched over her children constantly invades her, and at these times, she falls into a deep depression. The guilt is exceptionally hard when her husband blames her repeatedly for the children's drownings. At these times we the women, stand to support her in all we can. "We are like sisters, true to this and any difficult time."

After tending to her mother and wife's duties, Marina grows corn and vegetables in her large garden at the side of her house. It seems that her spirit of acceptance has grown by gardening. Eight years have passed, and life continues. Marina will forever live with the children in her heart and faith that she will see her children again.

Meeting Marina and finding out about her terrible ordeal touched me deeply. I feel great sympathy and a sort of connection with her. I am told that since the tragedy, she doesn't do much talking to anyone. Marina turned from a happy, talkative woman to a very deeply lost soul. She only leaves her house to visit the church or her children's tombs in the cemetery. The women in the compound respect her decision and hope she will return to being at least half of the Marina they knew one day. I watch Marina from afar in hopes of finding a way to talk to her or help her.

CHAPTER 40
LA MUDA DOROTEA

Today I saw "La Muda Dorotea" in the plaza. I had seen her many times before, and today I finally met her. Rafaela introduces us. Dorotea shakes my hand and gives me a big smile. She quickly excuses herself to continue her daily tasks of washing the church benches. It is then that Rafaela tells me Dorotea's life story.

"Doratea was born deaf-mute, and the village, not understanding her condition, always treated her like an outcast. Her parents are ashamed of her for her condition, believing she is a curse or some sort of bad omen. At seven years old, Dorotea was on her own. Her mother placed her to live alone in a shed with the farm animals. Dorotea very quickly learned to survive and manage. Her mother sometimes fed her leftovers, and when really hungry, she went to people's houses, where she asked for food. The whole village knows Dorotea. As a young unprotected child, it was easy for anybody, especially men, to take advantage of her. There was no law or anyone at the time to protect her. The women from the village treat her well and give her odd and small jobs to earn her keep. They give her old clothes whenever possible for her and her children."

"I am told that by her thirteenth birthday, due to her young age and malnutrition, Dorotea had two miscarriages that almost took her life. At the age of 15, she had her firstborn, a son, then a daughter a year later. Never knowing who the fathers were, the children are also ridiculed and considered to be batards by the people's ignorance. Dorotea somehow learned to communicate with grunts and hand gestures. Through Rafaela's translation, she told me of the day her mother sold her twin babies to a couple of strangers in the nearby town. Dorotea cried many nights for her children, and her mother has never given her an answer to who, why, or to whom she sold her babies. Dorotea has had a hard life and has learned to be a true survivor. She has never forgotten her children. She tells me she dreams and cries for them at times. Besides her life, she has women friends who help her. Dorotea always has a smile on her face."

"Dorotea had no other choice for survival but to give up her body for a few cents. This put tortillas and beans for her and her children. It wasn't until she went under the protection of the new town priest that the village respected her. The priest demanded that the villagers see her as their equal and that it was a sin not to. This made a great difference in her life. Dorotea is now in her late thirties, but looking at her tired face, you would think she was much older. Her hard life has left its prints on her face and body. Her face seems the keeper of much sadness. Ironically she continues to live each day with a smile on her face. Enjoying her children and the little that life offers her."

Looking at Dorotea, I could tell she is a sweet woman with a loving heart. She's very quiet and her mannerisms are warm and kind. Although aged I notice she acts somewhat like an innocent child. She smiles at the world, even if the world has wronged her. So far meeting and learning about Dorotea and Marina's tragic life makes me see the lightness of my own "tragedy" and journeys in my life. My pain is still real, but somehow I feel more fortunate than these two women.

Dorotea is still the village prostitute. That's no secret to everyone here. Dorotea has known nothing else. She knows well that all this provides food for her and her children. She continues her life here in La Laja, living what life as she knows. Nothing more and nothing less, but simply living. She walks in the plaza with great assurance and peace in her heart. She's like an angel walking on earth.

CHAPTER 41
CALLING HOME
OCTOBER 21, 1982

It's Sunday morning, and it has now been more than four weeks since I first arrived in La Laja. At times it has been hard or easier, depending on what is happening. I'm starting to feel temporarily disconnected from my family and world, which bothers me. I feel so far away, and like I'm on a whole new planet. In the last three days, I've had difficulty sleeping and thinking about all this. I especially miss my Friday morning visits to Xavier's tomb, where I feel at peace with him. The agreement is that I stay in La Laja for at least three months, but in the weeks since my arrival, I'm beginning to feel lonely and longing to be with my family.

During breakfast, I let Tia Maria know about how I miss my family, and how I'm anxious to be back home with them. Tia takes my hand and tells me she understands what I'm going through and that it is natural for me to feel this. "What can I do to feel better? I ask her." "You need always to learn to keep in mind three things, *one faith, two patience, and three, just belief.* "You need all three, emotionally, spiritually, and mentally to survive your journey." She then continues to explain: "*Faith* is to know that God is in charge of our lives and he always wants the best for us. *Patience* is trusting that everything we need comes always on his time, which is the right time and perfect time. *Belief:* *Believing* that God's magnificent love for us is real. And that all things, good or bad, happen for a reason. Knowing and believing in all these three things will always remind you that you are in God's hands and that you are safe there."

I listen to Tia with respect and admiration, for Tia is a wise woman, who's lived a long life and gone through many difficult situations. She has gotten her wisdom from her ancestors who mentored her. *"El diablo sabe más por viejo que por diablo."* She tells me with a direct smile on her face. *"The devil is wise because of his age, not because he's the devil."*

Seeing my desperation to call home, Tia Maria tells me, "I'll tell you what, why don't we go to Doña Lupe's little *tiendita* store and buy some phone time?" "Really? Is that possible?" I tell Tia Maria with a smile on my face. "Of Course it's possible," she tells me as she warmly takes my hand. "Who is Doña Lupe?" I ask. "She is the only person in the area with a phone, and for a few **pesos** you can use it on Sundays or in emergencies." " And you, my child, it's Sunday, and you have an emotional emergency right now." "Great! It's Sunday, and I know Jose is home with Eddie. This is a good time to call them," I tell her.

"The *tiendita* is at the edge of the village, it should take us 20 minutes to walk and get there. Then, afterward, we can go to the mid-day mass." Hearing this makes me happy. The fact that I can speak to Jose lightens my heart and I know hearing his voice will keep me going.

Once in Doña Lupe's *tiendita*, I nervously come in the door to pick up the phone and dial home. I can hear the phone ring three times and Jose finally answers. I hear a "hello," and I realize it's Jose. "Honey, is this you?" He asks. I didn't expect to cry, but I'm surprised I broke out into tears when I finally heard his voice again. "Is everything ok?" he asks. "Yes, everything is fine," I quickly answered him. "I just had to hear your voice again. I miss you and Eddie so much," I tell him. "And we miss you too," he tells me. "Every day, Eddie asks about you, especially at bedtime. He asks me when will you come back home? I tell him that Mama will be back soon." Tia steps outside the *tiendita* to give me a bit more privacy. I then get a chance to speak with Eddie, and my heart rejoices. "Mama, can you bring me a baby animal for a pet? Papa says that there are many baby animals where you are, can you bring me one on the plane, please!."

I can't help but smile at his innocent request. I hear Jose laughing in the background as he listens to Eddie. "Tia took me to Mcdonald's yesterday" , he says with delight. "Then she took me to the park to play on the swings''. Then he all of a sudden quickly said goodbye and gave the phone to Papa. I could then hear him running around the house, announcing that "Mommy is bringing me a baby pet!."

The phone call continued with Jose telling me how much he loves me and misses me. He tells me he's praying for me. I tell him the same. I tell him of all the people I have met so far, and of the silly stories on how hard it is learning to use the outhouse, "which you did not warn me about," I tell him. I also tell him about the Fiesta in the Plaza, Dorotea, and the tragedy of Marina's children. Our conversation continues for ten minutes until the limit for the phone call comes to an end. I say goodbye to Jose and I hang up. The phone call has given me new energy and a willingness to continue my journey here. From this Sunday on, I'll call home every other week before Sunday mass.

Chapter 42
The Old Woman In The Church

October 21, 1982

After making the phone call Tia Maria assures me that the future weeks here in La Laja will be better and very important for my learning. Although, for now not understand why? I am looking forward to what her words tell me. On our way to the church, Tia Maria explains that the surrounding villages share one priest in common and that Sunday mass is only held here every other week. "We look forward to attending Sunday mass every time it's offered." "It is our saving grace and social outlet every month for most of us."

Walking through the plaza I can see the small church at the very end. I have seen it twice from the outside, and today will be the first time I go inside.

Upon entering the small church, we encounter a small wooden fountain with holy water standing on the side of the entry door. We bless ourselves by dipping our index finger in the holy water and making the sign of the cross on our foreheads. Walking into the church, I soon recognize the different simple clay statues and paintings of saints placed up high on each side of the church's white-wash walls. I see the stages of the cross and the Holy Mother praying.

The church has ten old wooden benches on each side, freeing the center to see Dorotea sitting in the back with her two children. Then I see Rafaela and Marina sitting with their children on the front benches near the altar. The altar is a simple long table covered with a beautiful white hand-embroidered tablecloth with a large cross embroidered in the center. Some flowers are adorning it and what looks to be a simple gold crucifix in the center.

A strong smell of pine and incense invaded the church and my senses, giving me a feeling of holiness and peace. There are a few used candles lit at the altar. Some people are sitting and some standing by now. I see Elena and Regina sitting with their friends. Soon, the church bells ring, and a church song begins to be heard. Elderly women sing the song with angelic voices. I recognize the song from when my grandmother took me to Sunday mass in Guadalajara as a child. A second song soon begins and everyone in the church stands. The priest slowly walks in from the back door, and through the middle aisle, holding the bible until he reaches the altar. There, he steps up and begins the ritual.

Looking back I notice that most of the people attending mass are women and children. Very few men are present. Tia Maria finds a small space on one of the front benches for both of us to sit. From here, I can hear the women continuing their beautiful chanting much better. After a couple of welcoming church songs, the priest turns and faces the people and raises both hands, signaling the beginning of the mass. Then he leads the people in making the sign of the cross. "In the name of the Father, the Son, and the holy spirit." I listen to the priest attentively. It's been a while since I attended Sunday mass. I never could while living with my son in the hospital. And I have missed it.

The priest continues with the Our Father and Hail Mary. After a few minutes of prayer, the priest begins to preach the gospel for the day. The message is profound and it touches my heart. As I listen to the gospel, I also feel a sense of peace and tranquility in the church. I look up towards the ceiling and see three little angels floating and dancing above me. I'm reminded that I have a little angel in heaven.

Looking at the bench in front of me I notice an old brittle gray hair woman, surrounded by young children and sitting on the bench across from me. This caught my attention right away because of her worn-out clothes and because I had never seen her in the village in my weeks here. A total of six children sit together by her side. All seem to be below the age of twelve. A young girl about ten holds a small infant on her lap. The old woman constantly wipes tears from her eyes with her rebozo, and the children sit quietly in respect. All of the children are wearing old but clean worn-out clothing. Some of the children have no shoes, and the baby is wrapped in worn-out cloth. I could not help but stare at them for a minute and wonder their story. Such a sad sight so overtakes my heart.

After mass, the old woman and the children quickly left the church before I could come to meet them. They seem to be in a hurry, quickly walking off the church and magically disappearing in the plaza. "Who's the old woman with all the children?" I asked Tia Maria, as we entered the Plaza. Tia explains, "The old woman is the widow Doña Tomasa, who lives in an old abandoned house at the edge of the village." "About seven years ago, she and her small family came from another nearby village, on the other side of the mountain to live here. No one really knows much about them, as they are new to La Laja. "Who are the children?" I ask in curiosity. "They are all her grandchildren," Tia Maria answers.. "Why didn't the mother and father accompany them to church? And why are they so poorly dressed?" "That's because they are very poor," Tia answers me, "poorer than most of us living here." "A terrible tragedy left doña Tomasa alone to raise all her grandchildren alone." "What happened?'' I ask her with great concern. "Where are the parents?" We found a bench on the side of the plaza where we could speak in privacy. Once sitting, she began to tell me the story of Doña Tomasa and her grandchildren.

"Three years ago, the Widow Tomasa's only son Matias, being very poor, got an opportunity to go to El Norte (USA) and try to make some money to feed his family." " All we know about this family, Tia Maria continues, is that the family lost everything, their land, and home. And since they had no real way to make a living in their little village, they decided to come here hoping for a better chance of survival. But living here in La Laja, it became even harder for them to be here. For not owning your own land here, there is no work and much poverty here."

In desperation, Matias was convinced that he successfully cross the border to the United States. He heard that he, like many others, could somehow get some kind of a job there. Texas was where he knew some of his friends made it and lived there. And so that would be the place he would head to. He was convinced that there was no other way to take care of and feed his family.

Matias was the only man in the house. His father died when he was very young. He married young and was now in his teens and had five children, a pregnant wife, and a widowed mother to take care of. Matias saw no other way out, so they sold what little they had, to make his trip possible.

"His plans were to go to the state of Sonora in Mexico and there cross the border to Arizona and finally Texas. Many of his friends had made the same plans and made it there, and Matias hoped he'd have the same luck. Once he made it to Sonora, his plans were to hire a coyote to help him finally cross the border. He left home early one morning with his wife crying and his mother blessing him and praying for his safety.

"Weeks went by with no news from Matias. The days and weeks went by with no news again and again. Amparo and Tomosa are worried every day more and more about Matia's situation. Soon they became very nervous and worried and thought that by now something might have happened to him by now. They spent each minute of the day doing chores praying and lighting candles at church for his safety and fast return home. But no news came for days and then weeks. Amparo had no idea where or how to look for her husband. Amparo and Doña Tomasa became desperate for their situation.

One day news finally arrived. One of Matias' friends living in Texas contacted his relative in La Laja. The news was tragic for Amparo, Tomasa, and their children.

Matias had perished in the Arizona desert, in trying to desperately and unsuccessfully cross the border. The coyote in then abandoned Matias in the desert. Even worse, his body has not been recovered. This was terrible news! This tragic news made Amparo go into early labor and she delivered their 6th baby prematurely. By some miracle of God, the child somehow survived, but Amparo became very weak and sickly."

Tia Maria then continues the story, "A few weeks later after the news, Amparo and Tomasa had nothing left to feed the children. The village people of La Laja did what we could to help the family, but it was hard on everyone already. There had been very little rain and crops were scarce that year. Finally, a landowning farmer offered a sack of beans, rice, and corn to Amparo's family. All this was given with the understanding that she had to find a way to pick up the sacks and take them to her house on her own. It was a farming season and most farmers and farmhands were busy in the fields. The previous season had also been hard for everyone and they could not afford to leave one field unattended.

"Not having a horse or donkey or farm hand to help carry the sacks up the great hill to her house, Amparo decided to go and get the sacks on her own. Early one morning Amparo heads down the hillside with her eldest sons 5 and 7. She was determined to find a way to bring the sacks of food for the children up to her home. Amparo tried to get creative by using some small ropes to tie the sacks together and drag them on a sort of sled."

"Once tying the sacks, she and her small sons had the hard task of dragging and pulling the large sacks of food up the hillside. The boys did as much as their little bodies would allow. Until one of the sacks came loose and instead of leaving it behind, Amparo in her desperation and determination decided to pick up the heavy sack and carry it on her head and shoulders. The long road took hours in the hot sun."

"Finally, after all the long effort, they finally reached Amparo's house. The grandmother and children rejoiced at the sight of the sacs of food. This meant plenty of food for them for a few weeks, maybe months. Grandmother quickly made some rice and beans that very afternoon, and for the first time in many months, the children went to bed with a full stomach."

"But that very night, as the family headed to their only beds, Amparo complained to her mother-in-inlaw of having a strong and tortuous headache. Doña Tomasa quickly decided to go to the kitchen to make her some tea to help Amparo feel better. But when Doña Tomasa returned to Amparo with the tea, she found her very pale, cold, and unresponsive. Doña Tomasa called out her name and shook her, but Amparo did not respond. She was dying, it was too late. Amparo had suffered a brain hemorrhage and quickly died. The hemorrhage was believed to be caused by all the heavy lifting Amparo did in her weak state. Just like

Matias, Amparo risked her life to feed her children. And now Doña Tomasa and the children are all alone."

"Doña Tomasa is now in charge of the children and their livelihood. The children have adapted to their lives by learning to work in helping other farmers with their farming and their chores. This brings food to their table and their little family. Doña Tomasa and her two granddaughters clean houses and wash and iron people's clothes for food and some old clothing. They live in an old abandoned house loaned to them. And the people try to keep the children fed and safe as much as possible. Some villagers volunteered to take a child each to help Doña Tomasa. But the children don't want to get separated from one another. They rather live in poverty but together."

" And that is their story." Tia Maria tells me with great sadness. "We feel bad not to be able to give this family more. We are all poor here, but we do what we can with them."

At this moment, I don't know what to say or think. Knowing the story behind Doña Tomasa and the children leaves me numb. All I know right now is that I want to help make things better for them as soon as I can. My heart is broken for each and every one of them. Knowing this story and witnessing the children's and grandmother's sadness, makes me recognize and be thankful for all my blessings. I realize that my pain and mourning is much more bearable, compared to what this family is going through.

I came to realize that there are so many difficult situations in people's lives. I can see that tragedy lives everywhere, not only at the Children's Hospital of Los Angeles. The difference is that the people here move forward and continue to live their lives with love, patience, and somehow great belief and gratitude in their hearts. Doña Tomasa teaches her grandchildren all these virtues and this is how they learn to survive and accept their living conditions. They know that they have a love for each other and that's what matters. They know that their parents are watching over them from heaven. And believe that their lives will get better one day. They have faith that blessings will follow soon.

In La Laja I have come to see that children mature and grow quicker than they normally should or do in the cities or even America. Their life circumstances sometimes give them no other choice. They are resilient. Such is the case with my husband Jose. When he and his family lived in La Laja, poverty made them stronger and more accepting of life's fortunes or misfortunes. I feel saddened by the story of Doña Tomasa and her grandchildren, as I feel about Marina and her children, but I also see a great lesson and strength in this. The family's love and unity, are a prime examples of patience and belief, all these being part of love and faith in God and humanity. It seems to me that they somehow understand that their journeys in this life have a purpose.

Chapter 43
Flashback To 1977 Meeting Jose

October 24, 1982

After Sunday dinner I lay in my bed thinking about how much I miss Jose. I close my eyes to see his face in my mind. I then begin to remember the day we met.

One weekend, my schoolmate Marissa invited me to attend a family fiesta or *"Quinceanera."* At first, I was reluctant to go, claiming I had a lot of reading to do for a class, but my friend quickly convinced me to go and enjoy myself for at least a couple of hours. I quickly go through my closet, looking for something to wear and pulling out one of my favorite outfits.

When I arrive at the party, I find out that Marrissa has a hidden agenda behind her invitation. Once greeting me at the door, she takes me into the dance hall to introduce me to her cousin, but before she does, she mentions that he is a U.S. Army soldier who was visiting from his camp, and he saw a picture of me in her wallet and wanted to meet me. Marissa introduces me to her cousin, who is all decked or dressed up in his Uniform. I'm not very impressed by Martin. All he does is talk about himself, how good of a soldier he is, and how handsome he looks in his uniform. What a real ham! I quickly think to myself. This is a total turn-off for me. I can tell that Martin is trying too hard to impress me, and so far he is not being successful.

Soon Marissa sits us together at a table, and Martin continues talking about himself. I try very hard to listen to his stories about how brave and strong he is, and I can kick myself for listening to Marissa and coming here tonight. "I could have been studying," I say to myself, as I saw Martins' mouth moving but not hearing anything he said. Soon in my boredom, my eyes begin to wander around the dance hall. After a few minutes of looking around, I notice a quiet young man sitting alone at a table across from us. Something about this young man calls me and makes an impression on me, and I can't help but stare at him.

Soon Marissa returns to the table with some drinks and she sits and joins us. "Doesn't Martin look handsome in his uniform?" She asks me. "I guess," I answer, my eyes still fixed on the young man across from me. "Who is that sitting alone at that table across from here?" I ask Marrissa. "Oh, that's my brother Jose. She says. " He seems so quiet," I tell her. "He's probably in a bad mood because he broke up with his girlfriend last week." "Why are you asking me that question?" Marissa asks. "He looks like an interesting person to me," I answered her. "You think so?"

For the next ten minutes or so, I sat quietly and not saying much, and was not interested in Martin and Marissa's conversations. By now, both Marissa and Martin realize that their plan with me failed. I then decide to very cautiously and politely excuse myself to go to the lady's room. Marissa follows me there. Once in the lady's room, Marissa says, "I thought you might like Martin. "Sorry. But No I don't." I answer, "He's just not my type." "But you just met him, how can you tell?" "I just know things like this right away." "I'm sure he is a nice person, but he is not someone I would date." "I just wanted to get you interested in somebody," Marrissa tells me. "You need a companion. You are always so all alone." "I want to talk to your brother instead, I tell her," shocking her. "What? You want to meet Jose?" "Trust me, he is not a very interesting guy. Why do you think his girlfriend left him?" "Why would you want to meet him?"

"I don't know the answer, Marissa, I just think he looks safe to talk to." "All right my friend," Marissa tells me. "I'll introduce you to my moody brother, but don't blame me for anything that happens between you two later."

Leaving the lady's room Marissa finds a way to introduce me to Jose. "I warn you, she says to me, I think he still loves his ex-girlfriend Teresa." "No problem," I answered her, "I just want to be his friend, I don't have any love interest in anybody right now. " Or maybe I should just go home," I tell Marissa. "No, don't go, come with me." Marrissa takes me to the table and finally introduces me to her brother. "Jose, this is my friend from school, her name is Leticia." "Hello Leticia he says, nice to meet you." He says not really paying attention to me. "Nice to meet you" I answer him. "Can she join you at this table? There is no other place to sit here." "Fine" He answers with no real interest in mind.

Marissa quickly excuses herself to go over to Martin's table to explain the situation to him. But Martin, having had some drinks, is not ready for rejection. He says he is an Army Man, and he doesn't give up that easily! Marissa tries to explain again and to keep Martin from coming to my table.

Jose doesn't say much to me and just sips his beer and stares off at the dance floor. "Let's dance." Martin suddenly approaches me at the table. I turn to him and very nicely and politely answer, "No thank you. I don't feel like dancing." Martin insists by trying to take my hand and pull me to the dance floor. But I quickly pulled it away from him. "I told you I don't want to dance right now." Martin continues insisting. By this time Jose notices the situation between the two of us, and with a strong tone of voice, he tells Martin to stop bothering me. Martin tells him to mind his own business and tries to pull my hand once more.

Jose then stands up from his seat and says, " I said to leave her alone, stop bothering her, she doesn't want to dance!" Martin lets go of my arm and stands up to Jose. Hearing this commotion, Marissa quickly comes over and convinces Martin to go with her to meet someone else. Martin realizes that he doesn't want to argue with his own cousin and upset the family, so he excuses himself like a gentleman and follows Marissa to another table.

"Please forgive my cousin, Martin," Jose tells me, "he can be very forceful sometimes." " Ever since he joined the Army he thinks everyone should do as he says." "No problem," I say to Jose with a smile. "This is not the first time I meet someone like him," I told him. Jose looks closely at me and says: "I've seen you before, but I'm not sure where?" "I'm Marissa's friend from school," I answered him. "Oh that's why you look familiar," he says, "I've seen you come to the house before to study. "Would you like a drink or something?"

For the next two hours, we sat talking at the table like two good friends. Jose asked me about my college plans, and where my family was from. I told him we were from Guadalajara and he told me his family came from a small village two hours north of Guadalajara. Our conversation seemed to interest Jose and I was so happy to meet him. Marissa had succeeded in having me meet someone in her family, she just never thought it would be her brother.

The next few months Jose and I began dating and getting to know each other better. I learned that Jose was a simple caring man. He believes in living life simple and not complicate things. In getting to know me, Jose let me know that I was exactly what he was looking for in a woman, I found in him what I was looking for in a man. A year later we were married.

LOVE WAS YOU

I don't know why,

but when I saw you

Something inside me spoke

I asked myself, is that him?

Sitting at the table in my view

A gentleman you were with me

Your simple heart spoke

And from there on

We held hands

Till we grew old

10/77

Chapter 44
The Story of Our Wedding

October 28, 1982

The evenings in La Laja are used to relax with family and good company. Children play in the "patio" or courtyard. Men sit and talk about their harvests, the weather, and their animals. Women embroider or knit and talk about the day and what they do. I enjoy sitting with the women and listening to their talks. I learn many things about them and life in their conversations. They seem to be relaxed at the end of the day and free from the day's routine. This is something you don't see or live in a big city setting like Los Angeles. Life is too hectic in the city, and people don't seem to make it or have time just to sit and talk. On one of these evenings, the subject of discussion was how each couple met and how they married.

Rafaela begins by telling her story of how she and Manuel met and how they fell at age 14. They saw each other at the plaza and fell in love while attending church every Sunday. Every Sunday, Manuel would wear his Sunday best to church to impress Rafaela. Rafaela says she played hard to get until one day, he took a serenata to her window and sang to her. "That was the only occasion he's ever sung," she says. Everyone laughs. Soon he asked me for his hand in marriage, and I again played hard to get until I saw he was serious and began to build our little future adobe home. Then I took him seriously and accepted to marry him. "We had a modest church ceremony with just the family, which was the entire village." Everyone laughs.

Regina then tells her story. She explains how Antonio, a very handsome man, quickly convinced her to elope with him and to live with him unmarried. "I accepted because I thought he was so handsome and loved him too." "But not living as a married couple by the church broke my parents' hearts," Regina says she was especially afraid to face her father because he didn't believe Antonio would ever want to marry her through the church and that she would live in sin forever. And that Antonio would easily leave her for another woman that way. Marriage by the church was important to my father and most of the people in town. But to this day, Antonio has not asked for my hand in marriage.

After we eloped, my father swore to kill Antonio for taking me by force. My mother convinced my father that Antonio did not force anything on me and that I eloped with him by choice because I loved him. My father is still angry with Antonio for taking me. I was his little girl, and Antonio took me to live in another village. He still waits for Antonio to marry me in the town church. He tells me that all the time. Antonio tells me he doesn't need a church and priest to tell him how to love his wife, married or not. " At this point, I don't know what to do, she says. I love Antonio, and I love my father too."

Socorro tells her story. She begins by telling us how she was the one to convince Marcos to marry her. Everyone laughs. She continues, "Marcos was too shy to ask me to be his girl, so I asked him instead. Months passed, and I thought it was about time to get married, so I convinced Antonio to ask my father for my hand in marriage. Antonio being shy and quiet, had difficulty talking to my father, who is the opposite of him. "Much to Antonio's surprise, my father told him not only to take my hand but to take all of me completely."

" Antonio is and always will be shy. And this drives me crazy sometimes," she says. "But overall, I love my shy Antonio. To this day, Antonio tells me how my father gave me away to him. And that I completely belong to him."

"What a funny story I tell her." The women all laugh, and then it is my turn to tell my story. They asked me how I met Jose and about our wedding day. They want to hear the whole story of our wedding day first. And so I begin my story by telling them: "Jose and

I got married on a beautiful sunny December day. Our religious ceremony took place at a beautiful church named after the Blessed Mother Mary. NUESTRA SEÑORA DE GUADALUPE in Los Angeles. The church was filled with beautiful white flowers and white bows. The priest celebrated the mass in both Spanish and English. Our reception took place in a large community gymnasium. The basketball court was our dance floor, and the basketball stands served by holding our toilet paper-colored flower decorations that went from one side of the court to the other, and we also had *papel picado.*"

"What is a gymnasium?" Regina asked, "And what is a basketball court," Elena asked. The women all looked at me with curiosity. I explain as well and closely as possible, but I don't think they got it. Sports and basketball courts are something foreign to them. I continued my story by telling them, "Our friends could not believe we were having our wedding in a gymnasium." I told my friends that "the place did not matter to both of us. What mattered was that we would have all our family and friends with us celebrating our love." The women sigh. "Our tablecloths were paper clothes, something not done at weddings, but we did.

Jose and I were never into looking good for other people; instead, we did what was reasonable with our budget. "At our wedding, everyone seemed to have had fun and enjoyed themselves, which made it all worthwhile."

"We had a large wedding court, mostly all our brothers and sisters and close friends. The cost of the wedding was divided between the two families. My father paid for the mariachi playing at the church and during the dinner reception. Jose's father and mother were in charge of the food. Mexican mole with *sopa*. A real Mexican feast, complete with tortillas, salsa, and frijoles charros. It was all so perfect for Jose and me."

Then they asked about my wedding dress. I told them, "my wedding dress was a beautiful and simple gown designed by me and sewn by my mother." Regina jumps into the story to say, "I want to sew wedding dresses one day." "And you will," I tell her. Then I continue my story.

"It was a beautiful white lace dress with cream-colored pearls sewn all over the front of the dress in heart shapes. The back of the dress had a long strand of small round pearl-like buttons decorated over the lace and a long train. I wore my hair in a simple bun, and my ears I wore a pair of fake pearl earrings given to me by my grandmother." "You must have looked like a princess," Marina says.

"I felt like one for sure," I tell them. "I felt like a real princess that whole day." "I was very happy to have the love of my life with me finally." "That's a lovely story," Elena says, "it's just like a **novela** on t.v" "What did Jose wear?" Rafaela asks. "Jose looked very handsome in a black suit his father bought as a wedding gift."

"Jose and I were the first in both families to marry in church and to have a big celebration. The whole family was excited about this."

"Like most Mexican weddings in the U.S., there was plenty of food, liquor, and dancing. Family and friends met, some for the first time, and enjoyed themselves. The celebration had a live band playing Spanish songs which most of us knew and sang along to. I can say that our wedding was one of a kind and it was so incredible. This day lives in my memory as one of the happiest days in my life."

"Sounds like a storybook story," Regina says, "like a dream." "I want my wedding to be like that!" Elena says as she sighs and holds her hands together near her heart. "I'm sure you will have a beautiful wedding," I tell her as I reach for her hand.

CHAPTER 45
MANUEL AND RAFAELA

OCTOBER 29,1982

Rafaela is the quietest woman in the group. She doesn't speak much, and her real passion is cooking. She was taught to cook from a very young age by her grandmother and her mother. Rafaela cooks with passion and real love and has a story about each dish passed down from older generations. Rafaela strictly and respectfully follows the old traditional ways of cooking. She values the recipes that were created long before she was even born. Rafaela does most of the cooking for her family and at times, for the compound. She also takes it upon herself to teach the other women the secrets of the old recipes.

Rafaela and the other women of the family compound organize and cook the day's meals for the men and children. All three meals are prepared, starting with breakfast and ending with dinner. All women contribute by helping or taking turns cooking and setting up for the large family group. The family usually eats together, especially at the midday meal.

In the evening or whenever she has time, Rafaela also makes beautiful embroidery that she also learned from her mother. Her *servilletas,* pillow covers, and *manteles* are everywhere in the family compound. Everyone admires her beautiful needlework. She embroiders colorful flowers, trees, and animal figures by memory. She is very proud of her work and her contributions to the family.

Throughout my time here, Rafaela always has a lighted white candle sitting on a small stool in the corner of the long living room. A black-and-white picture of a teenage boy is on the wall above the candle. One day I decided to ask her for the meaning of this. "This is the picture of her son Omar, who died of stomach cancer." Hearing these words come out of her mouth; my heart skipped a beat. "What? You lost a teenage son last year?" Yes, Rafaela says, I miss my son, but I also believe that death is a part of life, and she accepts God's will.

"Lo que Dios mande." Her resignation in accepting the blows suffered by her son's illness is admirable to me. Rafaela's quiet and serene spirit intrigues me. She tells me that Omar's cancer was excruciating for him and, at the same time, for her as well. After cancer appeared in his stomach, it invaded his whole body within two weeks. Rafaela says that she saw how her healthy oldest son was quickly deteriorating, and she somehow found the strength to always continue by his side with a positive outlook as she tended to him on his deathbed.

Like Marina, Rafaela accepts the loss of her son as an inevitable part of life. Something I have come to admire and need to learn for myself. I can see now that the loss of a child is only understood by those that lose children. We share a common pain and bond. One that only we undertake and understand. I'm learning so much here in La Laja. I now begin to see and comprehend what Jose was talking about.

Although a hard-working man who always provides for the family, Manuel's demons come out occasionally when he drinks. In these times, married life is easy for Rafaela. Manuel, the oldest in his family, learned as a young boy to tend to his younger brothers' and sisters' needs before his. Both Rafaela and Manuel had no real childhood because of similar reasons. This is true for many of the people in the village as well.

As a young child of six, Like many other children, Manuel began working, helping in the fields with his father and grandfather. He says that by age 10, he worked like any other adult man, planting crops in all types of harsh weather conditions. Manuel worked long, hard hours in the planting and harvest seasons with very little sleep. He never had the chance to go to school and had no free time to play as some children did. Manuel was introduced to alcohol by the men he worked with very early in his life.

In early dark and cold mornings, it is a custom to drink hot *canelas* or "cinnamon tea" with alcohol to keep workers warm and full of energy to make the most of the early morning labor. As a very young child, Manuel began to drink just like the men, and it never stopped. Rafaela struggles with her husband's demons and depression that are living inside her husband, and she doesn't know how to help him.

In the short time that I've been here, I have come to learn by now that for some men, alcohol is a common thing here, and it seems like no one addresses this issue with a solution. It seems that way at least for those suffering, that they have just learned to live with it.

Manuel and Rafaela have learned early in their lives to do as they need to to provide a survival lifestyle for themselves and their families. Aside from occasional drinking, Manuel is a generous and giving man. He is a role model to follow in his work ethic, a hard worker, and a provider. Manuel and Rafaela love and respect one another, which is a living example of a good marriage.

CHAPTER 46
COOKING AND DANCING LESSONS

OCTOBER 30,1982

One morning, I awoke as always, to a warm wood-heated bucket of water with which I could bathe. I dress and go to the kitchen for my daily breakfast. Now the women believe I should learn to do some kitchen duties. They explained to me that to be a real woman, I need to know what they all learned as children "to cook." They first teach me to churn the corn to make the masa *(nixtamal)*. The **masea** is made from churning kernels of corn by hand every morning for the day's fresh tortillas. Hand churning with the "*molino*" or hand grinder is very difficult. The first five minutes were fine, but then my arm and shoulder cramped. After a few minutes of churning, I began to complain of pain and gave it up.

"Tortillas are very special to us," Regina tells me. "They have and are always a part of our daily meals. At times tortillas are our only meal." my mother-in-law said to me that for generations, tortillas were made by hand and over a wooden li**t "comal"** or griddle on a stove. I now realize hand-made tortillas are still very much the case here in these households and the villages. The young girls are taught to *"tortear"* or make tortillas at a very young age. Once a young girl conquers this particular task or art of making tortillas, they are considered ready for marriage. "*Ya torteas, ya te puedes casar.*"

I find these tortillas to be incredibly delicious. I am enchanted with the smell and texture of tortillas cooking over the **comal** (griddle). Marina and Rafaela are in charge of making the tortillas for the day *(tortear)* and teaching the younger girls to do so. Regina and Socorro asked if I would like to learn to make tortillas. At first, I was reluctant and somewhat afraid to do something wrong on such an important task like this. I am not interested, I tell them, but the women insist on at least for me to try to make one. I agreed to try to make them feel better.

After washing my hands in the **"lavadero"** the women give me a *"mandil"* or apron, and a small ball of **masa**. They begin by placing the masa between the palms of my hands. I follow the women's directions and their modeling and begin to move a sort of applause with the maza. I try to make the masa stay in my hands, but I soon fail miserably. Then I try to form a round shape with the masa and again fail. This is a true art learned by these women in no time. The first four or five efforts result in triangular and rectangular shapes disasters. They were anything but round. The women giggle at my awkwardness and point to the odd shapes I created.

With Rafaela's help, I can finally form an oval kind of shaped tortilla and place it in the **comal** to cook. The women and children seem to be entertained by my actions or intentions. They say they have never seen such a shape in a tortilla before and laugh. Soon the biggest thrill for them came in my best performance as a *"torteadora."* This came when one of my acrylic nails gave a short spark when it got too close to the wood fire. When it happened, I was trying to turn the tortilla over in the very hot comal. This is the best part of my intentions of making tortillas.

The children wanted an anchore more! more! They ask me to turn the tortilla again with my other hand to see the small fireworks coming from my fingers. That was the highlight for me learning to make tortillas that day. I know the ladies and children will never forget this; it will probably be around town in no time.

I then explain to them, "In all my life, I have never enjoyed cooking or even being in the kitchen for more than what it takes to serve cereal and milk and leave. And I am not about to try cooking a meal now. I'm not made for such a thing. Cooking has never appealed to me," I tell the women as they look at me, not understanding why a woman doesn't enjoy cooking.

"Jose does most of the cooking at home," I tell them. "He enjoys it and seems to have a passion for it." On hearing this, the women's eyes open wide and simultaneously ask, "Jose does the cooking?" " Yes, I answer them" They look at me in disbelief. "I never heard of such a thing," Regina says. "A man doing the cooking?" The look on their faces is by now entertaining to me. I see the women wondering and asking each other what that could mean. A man doing the cooking instead of the woman? They giggle at this, still in disbelief. "But all women are supposed to cook," they tell me again. "From the time we are little girls we are taught by our mothers and grandmothers to cook, not the men." Regina insists. "The men have other duties."

"It is our duty as women to carry this tradition and cook for the men, not the other way around," Elena adds. "That's the law." "I'm sorry," I try to explain to them, "but times have changed, and life is different today. This law is not true anymore, at least not for me or many of the women living in the cities. Many women work outside the home and have other responsibilities to the family. Men help by sharing women's chores, like cooking and cleaning." "Cleaning," Tia Maria joins her comment to the group. "I never thought that day would ever come."

"In the cities, men and women share chores because, in most cases, both have to work to maintain a roof over their heads and food on the table." "In the cities, men are not the sole providers. Women have joined them too; therefore, it is not uncommon for men to cook and women to work."

"What kinds of things do you do for your family then?" They ask. "I do many other thighs but cook," I tell them. " I went to school and studied to be a teacher and a counselor. Most of my time is spent working with people". I understood the women's reactions, and I try to be respectful in my explanation.

Socorro then asks, "What do you do when you're hungry?" The women giggle. "Well like I told you, Jose does most of the cooking, and we go out to restaurants on special occasions to eat." Regina and Socorro laugh again, " We never heard of such a thing. Restaurants are for the rich people." "Are you rich?" "No, we are not rich, but in the city, anybody could go out to eat at a restaurant, or anywhere they sell food."

"But not all women are like me. There are lots of women in the city who enjoy cooking just like you. I just happen not to like or enjoy cooking, that's all. Some of us in the city are lucky to have a choice."

"Yes, you are so lucky," Elena says, "I wish I could live in the city and have a choice not to cook." "I want to be a teacher like you," she says. "To be a teacher is my dream." "Good for you!" I tell Elena, "I can see your love for teaching when you're around the children. You are already a teacher," I tell her. "We never had a teacher in the family," Socorro says. "Can you teach us something? Can you be our teacher?"

"I like the kitchen," Rafaela says. It fulfills my life, and I'm happy doing it. I'm very proud of it." "Good for you," I tell her, "You have a gift for cooking wonderful food and sharing with everyone. I can see that everyone loves and respects you for it." "This is my dream," Rafaela continues. Cooking keeps me happy." "I, too, say, Marina." Marina says quietly, "I enjoy cooking for my family too." "And you do very well, too," I tell her. The women smile.

"Cooking is a wonderful gift to have and to share with everyone. You are all very good at what you do. Everyone is born with a gift in their journey in life. All of you should be very proud of what you have with your gifts. Whether it's in the kitchen, sewing, teaching, helping women have babies, and knowing how to help people get better through your knowledge of herbs, "yerbas." All of our gifts feed our soul and the souls of others."

" I can tell you are a good teacher. You say good things," Marina says to me. "I admire what you do." Marina's kind and serene words overtake me. "And I admire and respect what you do," I tell Socorro. "Thank you," Socorro says. "Your words of admiration make us feel proud and important."

"And you are all so critical." "As important as the men and children working in the fields who grow the crops for you to cook. It's a beautiful perfect circle of life." "No one ever said anything like this to us," Regina adds. "I have never thought that what we do is as important as what men do in the fields' ' says Socorro.

"It is called survival," Tia Maria says. "The design of our lives is for surviving as a family and as a group. That is why every part of the cycle is important. That is why we teach our young children the trades to persevere in this life. God gives us everything we need to do so," Tia Maria says with great pride.

"I like to sew," Regina says. "I hope to one day get a sewing machine to make dresses and shirts for everyone." "What a noble thing to do," I tell her. "I'm sure you will soon have a sewing machine, and you will do just that."

"I have seen that all of you have admirable gifts and contributions for the family and society. For example, Rafaela, besides cooking, you like to knit and embroider beautiful things. I see them in the kitchen, the bedrooms, and everywhere in the compound. Elena, you like to teach. The children love to play games and learn from you. You, like me, are a natural teacher. We were born to teach."

"Socorro, Marina, and Regina, you like planting and growing beautiful things like flowers and vegetables. And Regina, you have the gift of helping mothers give birth to their children. What a wonderful gift.

" Do you teach little children how to read and write?" "No, not really," I tell them. I teach young teens and adults to read and write English and sometimes dance."

"To dance!" Regina shouts. "I want to learn how to dance!." "Can you teach me?" " Me too'' says Socorro, "and me!" Elena adds.

"Of course, I can teach you to dance." "When can we start?" Socorro anxiously asks. Regina says, "Can we start tomorrow?" I tell them all I must do is find some music records and a record player.." "Manuel has a record player," Rafaela says. " And my husband has some Mariachi records!" Socorro adds with delight. "I want to see what your dancing looks like. Regina asks. "Show us." "Right now?" I ask them with surprise. Yes!!! The woman answered right now.

I open my arms to simulate a wide dancing skirt and throw it in the air as in waves and loops and sing a song. 'How beautiful," Tia Maria says as she stands up from her chair and begins to copy the movements. "I used to dance when I was a child," she says, and "I still remember some of the moves I was taught." Tia Maria opens her arms and begins to swing around, and soon we both are dancing.

"I want to do that too," Elena says, and she too stands and begins to copy the dancing moves. Soon Regina and Socorro follow. Suddenly the kitchen became songs and dancing. Rafaella and Marina watched and smiled from the corner of the kitchen. They were too shy to join but enjoyed watching. *This was the first dance class I gave to* the women in La Laja. I didn't learn to make tortillas in the kitchen and in the middle of the day.

CHAPTER 47
THE MOUNTAIN
OCTOBER 31, 1982

It is a cold October morning, and Antonio's wife Regina and Socorro invite me to accompany them to the mountaintop to collect herbs, plants, flowers, *"cempasuchitl"* for the upcoming altars for Dia de Los Muertos. They are also collecting herbs for their healing tonics and teas, and I'm very interested in learning many things on this little adventure.

It is still dark outside, and the morning dew is fresh. Socorro explained to me the night before that going to the mountain early in the morning is very important. She also told me that this is the perfect time of the year to go to the mountain and collect herbs and plants. Especially the wild herbs that only grow this time of the year.

Getting up so early in the morning is quite a challenge for me, but I'm looking forward to this new and valuable adventure. I am told that Socorro's mother, grandmother, and great-grandmothers before her have been healers. *"Herb healers" curanderas* for this and surrounding villages for many years. These women's knowledge of medicinal herbs, *"yerbas"* serve a great purpose in the village and its surrounding neighbors. Medical attention is hard to come by in these places, and so there is a great need for *"curanderos."*

I am told by Tia Maria and Tio Juan and my mother-in-law back home that people have depended on curanderos for their medical health needs for generations. And that these needs range from a simple stomach ache to animal bites, fevers, and childbirth. They tell me Regina inherited this trade and knowledge from her mother, grandmother, and ancestors. These men and women, *"curanderos"* are well respected and trusted because of their wisdom. I am looking forward to my trip to the mountain. I've been invited to come along to help collect the herbs and roots they need and to try to learn about some of the basic medicinal recipes of herbs for my knowledge.

As I get ready, I can hear the women talking outside my window, and by now, I know they are waiting for me to come out of the house. As I step out of the door, I see both women carrying large empty baskets in their hands and say *"Buenos dias"* as I'm handed one of the baskets.

"Are you ready?" They ask me with a bit of wit. "Yes, I am!" I reply with real excitement and anticipation. The women also hand me a walking stick to use for guidance, they say. "It will help you scare off snakes and small animals," they tell me, not looking at me to see my surprised reaction. My eyes go wide open then and Socorro giggles.

We now begin to walk towards the mountain. Regina and Socorro are used to walking in the early morning darkness, but I'm not, so I struggle a bit, and I make sure not to stay far behind. People in the village have learned to wake up at the break of dawn to work in the fields and carry out their daily labor. And so they are accustomed and can easily find their way through the partial darkness of the morning.

Regina and Socorro know the *"veredas"* or small hidden back roads that lead them to the mountain very well. They have been walking these small roads with their elders since childhood. Regina leads the way while Socorro and I follow behind.

By now, I can hear the crunching of leaves and feel the small branches underneath my feet as I walk. I use the guiding stick to move some dry bushes and tree branches that are on my way. Soon I can hear the water running down the nearby creek. The morning's freshness soon soothes my already wet forehead. I also hear the birds singing as if reciting songs to one another. This experience is so very new to me. Nature and its majesty waking up to a new day. I consider myself very lucky to have this opportunity, which is one in a lifetime.

For the first time in my life, I'm experiencing and enjoying nature in its full surroundings in a very unique way. I can feel my son Xavier here. I believe that he is pleased. I feel he's among these trees, the running creek, and the singing birds. The different fragrances of the forest begin to wake all my senses. The strong smell of the pine and maple trees tells me that God and the angels live here.

"We are almost at the top of the mountain," Regina says. By now, I can begin to feel the upward climb to the mountain. My breathing is changing to deeper breaths. Regina asks me if I need to take a little rest before reaching the top. I answer, "Maybe later when we get up higher in the mountain." We then continue our hike upward as the morning light begins to break through the trees, and we welcome a new day.

After another few minutes, I now can tell that my body needs a break, and I tell them. By now my breathing is very heavy, and my legs are beginning to cramp. "Let's rest here," Regina points to a big rock. I sit by the big rock and try to take control of my breathing. I begin to admire the small animals coming out in the surrounding area to say hello. The little rabbits and squirrels, birds, and some deer passed by. After a few minutes of rest, we decided to continue our journey to the top.

Upon reaching the mountain top, I'm amazed at what my eyes see. I can't believe such beauty is absolute beauty. The majesty of nature in full glamor and bloom appears right before my eyes. Rows and rows of different colored flowers decorate the mountain. The trees and flowers softly sway from side to side as if greeting us. They seem to be slow dancing with the wind and its rhythms.

The different fragrances also offer a sense of peace and serenity up here. I now see Socorro and Regina putting down their baskets, spreading their arms outward and upward to the heavens, and singing a song of gratitude to the mountain. Regina's grandmother taught her to sing these songs as a child. She was told to always, before taking anything from the mountain, one has to thank and sing to the mountain for her bounty and for what she has to offer.

Spinning in circles and moving with the wind, the two women seem to be in a sort of magical transformation or trance. Their moves are joyful and peaceful at the same time. As I sit beside the tall grass, I also find peace in this mountain and especially with these women whom I now feel like one of them now. I see and feel them as my sisters. This kind of peace has been foreign to me for so long. Tears begin to run down my cheeks, these are tears of happiness and extreme joy. I then slowly stand, raise my arms to the heavens, and dance in the new sunlight, just like my sisters.

Once nature is thanked for its gifts and abundance, Regina begins by pointing out the basic herbs to me. "This is *Yerbabuena, Istafiate, and ruda,* all these are used for digestion or stomach problems," she says to me. Then she introduces me to other herbs and flowers and their different characteristics and functions. This is all so interesting and new to me. I want to take everything in and keep it.

Socorro points out a soft and small purple flower or "lavender." "These flowers have calming energies for tensions and nerves and they help you sleep," she says. We soon begin to fill all our large baskets with a combination of large and small leaves, stems, and flowers. I truly admire the natural knowledge and wisdom these women have and share with me. It is admirable to know that everything they bring down from the mountain will help the people in the village.

Regina then hands me an empty sack and asks me to fill it up with wildflowers, *"mansanilla" which are vastly growing and* used as teas in childbirth. She explains that these flowers are to help the unborn baby properly place itself in the uterus for delivery. It also helps the mother relax and have an easier delivery.

"What a wonderful thing to have available to the baby and mother," I say to Regina. "This is something I wish I knew this when I delivered my boys." "There is a cure for everything in these mountains," Regina tells me. "God, in his magnificent love for us, provides through nature everything we need." "Our ancestors told us that we must never forget this."

"The sad thing is that more than half of the Yerba or herbal knowledge has been lost. People leave the countryside to live in big cities and forget about all this." Socorro explains sadly. "People have turned to man's medicine and forgotten about the mountain and its gifts." My grandmother once told me that these days would eventually come, and I think they have come too fast," says Socorro.

" It's almost mid-morning, and It's time to eat," says Socorro as she pulls out some bean tacos and fruit from her basket. "I'll get some fresh water from the creek," Regina says as she carries a small container with her. Soon we three sit quietly and share a wonderful meal. We sit and eat quietly in a sort of communion with each other and nature. I now gradually begin to understand what Jose has been trying to tell me all along. No one could ever give me what this mountain and these people are giving me. My grief feels lighter and I'm learning to look at life for what it is. A gifted love.

THE MOUNTAIN

The Beauty of the Mountain Speaks

And tells her story

Her job is to always give to humanity

What God gave her in glory

The bounty of the mountain speaks in living, breathing colors

The forest, its mountain creeks, and flowers

Each walking hand in hand with one another

The answers are here, in every

Stem, flower, root, or leaf

And will forever be

If we believe, respect and Love her

The Mountain will always give us what we need

To help heal one another

If we only stop, listen, and truly believe

What the Mountain Top

And God offer

CHAPTER 48
DIA DE LOS ANGELITOS
NOVEMBER 1, 1982

Today is November 1st *"Dia de Los Angelitos"*
Today we celebrate the life of our little ones, who came
to join us for a bit on earth and then went to heaven.
The preparations for this day begin very early in the
morning. Everyone, including the men and children, is
involved in doing something for this event. Elena is in
charge of organizing the decorations.

Marina, Rafaela, and I work on making colorful
"papel picado" which will decorate the children's
tombs and cemetery. Regina has brought down many
beautiful flowers back from the mountain. Everyone else
is making beautiful paper mache bouquets and
arrangements for the tombs. Marina is making two
beautiful crowns for her children. She uses bright yellow

margaritas and **"cempasuchil"** flowers. "Cempasuchil '' is the flower used for the dead on these special days. I also decided to make a crown for Xavier, using beautiful white baby breaths and *cempasuchil* flowers.

Food for this occasion is fundamental. A special food feast is made to occur at nightfall in the cemetery. Rice, beans, and particular **"moles"** are made from old traditional recipes. Mexican sweet bread and fruits are also made and gathered for the ceremony/celebration.

Most of the day is spent on getting things ready. The men make some small wooden tables to be used as altars. They also sweep and clean the tombs, preparing them for the decorations the women make. The last thing the women do once everything is done is to get the pictures of their deceased children and decorate the frames. I searched through my wallet and found a small picture of Xavier in his hospital crib to decorate. I decided to place the picture in a small wooden frame given to me by Rafaela and decorated it with colorful flowers.

It is late afternoon. Although the water was more cold than warm, I have just taken a bucket bath, and I am getting dressed and ready to begin the pilgrimage to the cemetery. Everyone seems to be ready as I walk out the front door. The procession is to take place from the family patio to the cemetery.

Soon the procession is ready to begin. Everyone carries candles and flowers. The mothers carry their loved ones' pictures and cover their heads with rebozos as respect. I too cover my head and join the line next to Marina who gladly makes space for me to join them. Now the walk to the cemetery begins. Two inlines form with the women leading in the front. Other people in the village join as we pass them. The women begin to sing as we begin to leave the village and plaza and walk through the dirt road that leads us to our destination.

Men carry the torches that light the dirt road. My heart is pounding by now. The unity and love in the procession are something so surreal. Something I had never seen or felt before. I didn't feel alone in my grief. The company of people was comforting.

Everyone in the procession has lost a little one, and tonight all of us special parents join in celebrating together to remember and celebrate the time our little angels lived with us. Tears begin to invade my cheeks. My emotions are high, just like everyone else's. The beauty of this night is that everyone has had the same journey. I feel my pain is less when it is shared with other grieving family members and parents.

" We never forget our little angels," Tia Maria tells me with a tender smile. "They chose us from heaven to be their parents. They come to teach us many lessons, then leave to go back to heaven." My heart feels relieved and satisfied when I listen to her words. *My son chose me from heaven. What a beautiful thing.*

The procession continues, all by candlelight, some with torches and some with songs. All mothers are carrying a decorated picture of their child or children in their hands. The smell of the *cempazuchitl* flowers and candles   combined with the night excites my senses and sends chills down my spine. I can't help but tear up at what I see. The site is like a beautiful mystical dream to me. By this time, I can feel my son's love and energy all around me. I look at Marina and see tears in her eyes but a soft smile on her face. She then touches my hand, and our universe turns to one.

When finally reaching the cemetery, everyone in the small group walks towards the children's section and decorates the little tombs. There is a small graveside for the children who have no graves. I'm led there by Dorotea and I placed Xavier's picture and the crown that I made for him with a little wooden cross. Dorotea places a large bouquet for the children she lost. By now everyone is decorating their tombs and placing their pictures on them. The torches and candles are placed strategically to bring light to this beautiful celebration of remembrance.

Soon the men bring out and set the table for the food. A sumptuous feast is set in celebration. Sweet bread and fruit are placed in the tombs along with the flowers. Some mothers bring baby blankets and bottles for their babies. The night is filled with love, an actual and happy moment to embrace in the soul of a mother and child. I see some people beginning to eat. The small children run around playing games around the tombs. Songs and guitar music follow.

Hours go by, and by then it's time to leave and return to our homes. The decorations stay for the new day. I leave with the women of the compound. After this experience, I truly feel like one of these women. Again they are my sisters. All are a special part of something so grand, personal, and beautiful for me. *"I am one of them" "Like so many on the planet"* There is a real connection between us all. A genuine sisterhood and brotherhood boarded here today, and I know it will stay in me for the rest of my life. *Like a pile of sand, every grain of sand is different but the same.*

CHAPTER 49
DIA DE LOS MUERTOS
NOVEMBER 2, 1982

After yesterday's celebration of *November 1st "Dia de Los Angelitos,"* today I find it hard to wake up this early. The night before was long, and today I feel I need more sleep. But by now, I can hear the hustle and bustle happening outside my window, on the patio, and mostly in the kitchen. Then I remember today is a special day too, the **"Dia de Los Muertos"** celebration! I quickly spring up from my bed and get ready for the day.

Today is Dia de Los Muertos, the second celebration of the dead. Yesterday was the day of the angels or the children, which took a toll on my energy. Today is the celebration of all the dead, family, and friends who passed and left us.

Coming out of the house, I see the same scene as yesterday. Paper decorations being made, flowers bundles and decorations and most of all the making food. Regina tells me that today a large altar is being set and prepared in the plaza for all the townspeople to decorate with incense, flowers, and pictures of their loved ones.

At the end of the day, everyone in the village meets in the plaza and contributes to the community altar. The townspeople pray a rosary for their deceased family members and friends. Then, at nightfall, the pilgrimage begins from the plaza to the cemetery. On the way to the cemetery, just like the day before, songs are sung, and the music is lively. I can see that more people are attending this celebration than yesterday. People from different villages join the procession and the event is even more glorious.

Once arriving, the whole cemetery lights up with torches. And the decorations, flowers, candles, and pictures are placed in the individual tombs. The deceased's favorite foods and drinks are also placed there, and the meals are shared with everyone. This glorious and magnificent scene so overtakes me. The place lights up like daytime, and I can see each tomb's colors, shapes, and names.

"It is a common belief that on this night, our loved ones who passed on come back to visit with us and celebrate life and death with us." Tia Maria explains. "They come tonight to remind us that they are still with us."

The music is lively by now, with people singing. Looking around, I see so many candles illuminating the night in a heaven-like spirit. The flickering of the lights seems to be dancing and also celebrating with us. I stand back to enjoy the beautiful sight and realize that death is seen and felt differently here. No matter how tragic, death is seen with the idea of one day being back together again. "Today, Dia de Los Muertos is a special day. The dead are never forgotten here." Rafaela comes close and whispers to me. "We will always remember them because they live in our hearts." She says, "Tonight, we relive the moments and our memories with them here."

I walk towards the little tomb where Xavier's picture is and take him some flowers. I genuinely feel he is here and very content. In thinking about his short life and departure to heaven, I believe it was all meant to be. Now I know that I will see him again. I will hold him in my arms and kiss his little face again and forever. I also remember little Gabriel tonight and honor him. Everyone honors their loved ones, from great-grandparents to young children. For me, it is a really special honor to be here tonight. I also remember my grandparents and family and friends who passed on. This unforgettable scene will live within me forever.

CHAPTER 50
LAS POSADAS
DECEMBER 17, 1982

It will be Christmas Eve in a few days, *"La Noche Buena."* This has been a tough month for me to be away from my family, especially my son. In Mexico during this time, *"Posadas" are very popular with everyone. This is when everyone participates and when* the children have the most fun. At this time, I wish Eddie was here to enjoy and be a part of this tradition.

Even though I speak with Jose and Eddie on the phone every other week, it's not enough to fill my heart. I miss them both so much. The experiences and stories here have slowly begun to give me inner peace, but not enough to be satisfied with being away from my own.

I remember last Christmas when I was almost nine months pregnant and dreaming of having my second child. Eddie and Jose decorated the tree and the outside of the house. I never thought I would have lost a child the following Christmas and be without my son and husband in a faraway place like La Laja. Christmas has always been one of my favorite holidays, where family and friends gather to celebrate. And right now, it's not such a good Christmas for me.

All my years in the U.S., I had forgotten about *"Las Posadas"* from my early childhood years in Guadalajara. These were happy times for all children. My cousins and neighbors were always a part of this beautiful tradition and celebration. Christmas for most Mexicans begins December 15 with Las Posadas. This is a re-enactment of when the blessed family, Jose, and Maria were looking for a place to rest and for Maria to give birth to baby Jesus.

The nine days are organized between everyone in the family and neighborhood. Each family hosts a small feast every night. It begins with a small pilgrimage for everyone, even children, singing and holding candles and visiting the front doors of each house. Once the host family accepts the pilgrimage, the fiesta begins. There is usually a pinata and treats for the children, *Bunuelos, and colaciones.* The hosts typically serve tamales or posole with atole to their visitors. People look forward to these nine days of celebration. The children are taught the story of Jose and Maria looking for a place to rest and sleep. They also learn songs like the famous pinata song *"Dale dale dale."* I know Eddie would love *"La Posadas"* if he were here. I can't wait to bring him here to experience this.

CHAPTER 51
THE LAST POSADA
DECEMBER 24, 1982

Tonight, Manuel and Rafaela host the posada in their small home. It is Noche Buena, and they have prepared a tasty posole for dinner with all its trimmings. Rafaela made delicious Bunuelos and sweet tamales. Elena and the children made a beautiful star shape *piñata* and filled it with tangerines, oranges, peanuts, and candy. It's wonderful to see everyone participating and having a good time doing so. I find myself fully involved in such a way that I tend to forget my sadness.

Like all the women in the compound, I, too, have helped each host family make colorful *"papel picado"* decorations and *piñatas.* Each day is a special day where I come to learn not only about this tradition but also about the generosity that each host family has, of giving what little they may have to one another. I see the children enjoying singing the Posada songs and, most of all, enjoying the Pinatas. They all sing going from one house to another. I see that everyone's participation is important in this event, from the very young to the very old.

Tonight is December 24. Tomorrow is Christmas. The holy celebration today will continue with food, music, and dancing. The women make sure that I get involved in anything and everything they believe I can do, and I am starting to feel their love through their teachings and my participation.

La Noche Buena in Mexico is really unique. I have fond memories of my childhood in my old neighborhood in Guadalajara. I remember celebrating with my friends and family. My childhood feelings of freedom and love have returned to me during this holiday and are very much alive in me now. I remember getting gifts from Baby Jesus in my shoe. And the

happy mornings playing with my cousins. FELIZ
NAVIDAD.

CHAPTER 52
LA NAVIDAD
DECEMBER 25, 1982

The morning of December 25th, the children wake up eager to see what gifts Baby Jesus or " *El Niño Jesus'* has brought to their shoes. From an early age, the children are taught to believe that baby Jesus brings a little something to in their shoes or *huaraches*. I am amazed to see the children happy with the little they get. An apple or orange, some nuts or peanuts, animal cookies, and maybe a small plastic or homemade wooden toy.

People don't have much here. The parents are grateful for being able to provide their children with a little something as Christmas gifts. There is very little money for toys and things like that, but the children seem to be happy anyway. Their faces light up with the fruits, nuts, and animal cookies. There is no fuss about not getting them the latest toy or doll.

I have experienced so much through the Posadas and Christmas celebrations here in La Laja. I see that children and adults can be grateful for so little. I believe that this is the real meaning of Christmas. The birth of Baby Jesus and the giving of love. For some people, Christmas in Los Angeles is missing the part of family, unity, and love. It gets lost somewhere in the glamour and buying the latest gift.

This has been for me a true *"Feliz Navidad"* or Merry Christmas. The Christmas dinner will take place towards the end of the day. Women prepare the food while the children play with their little homemade gifts. Everyone seems so joyous. Even the men seem to enjoy this time of year. Everyone looks forward to the big feast on the large patio table for later.

CHAPTER 53
XAVIER'S FIRST BIRTHDAY
JANUARY 1, 1983

Today would have been Xavier's first birthday. My heart feels sad remembering the day he was born and all that happened afterward. I have spent most of the morning inside my room, sitting in my small bed and staring at the small window in the corner. I miss my baby so much. My arms have always felt empty since he left me, and today without Eddie near me, my arms feel incredibly empty. I had forgotten this feeling for a while, but here it is again.

I had briefly forgotten this feeling

And here it is once again

Since you left my arms,

They haven't been the same

I held you for so long,

That at times like this, feel empty and dead

your breathing echoes in my heart

And in my head,

Today is your first birthday my son

The birth that changed my life, forever and again

Feliz Cumpleaños

January 1, 1983

Xavier's First Birthday

January 1st is Xavier's birthday and I celebrated it with a private and quiet walk down the river bed. It is a beautiful afternoon, and I spent most of the day speaking to him and telling him how I miss him. I feel his presence in this beautiful place. The birds are singing, and a soft, warm wind is moving the trees.

I miss him so much today. I remember the first day and night we spent together in the hospital room, where he quietly slept in my arms. My sweet little baby was my everything and still is.

What was supposed to be a short walk turned into a long one. In my thoughts, I lost track of time. Almost two hours passed and I figured the women were worried about me. I begin to walk up the river bed to return to the compound, and I quickly see two figures coming down the road. It's Elena and Regina who come looking for me. "We were worried about you," they say. " Are you alright?" " Yes." I tell them. "I just needed to take a walk alone. It has been a peaceful and joyful walk," I assure them. "I'm happy for you," Elena said. "We know today is your son's birthday. We know how special he and this day are to you. "We believe that people born on the first day of the year are special messengers of God." "They come to bless our lives for the rest of the year in more ways than one," Regina adds. And I agreed. We then start heading back home, walking quietly up the road. "We collected flowers this morning to make a little birthday altar for Xavier." Elena says.

Reaching the house, I see a beautiful surprise. It's Xavier's birthday altar, a beautifully set up table in the middle of the patio made by the women and children. A wooden table covered with white satin-like cloth, specially embroidered with a holy cross of Jesus for little baby angels like my son. Different colored flowers decorate the altar, and one white candle stands lit in the middle of the small table.

"Little altars like these are an old tradition for someone no longer with us and it's their birthday." I was pleased with this simple and touching memorial honoring my son. Soon I would return home and somehow, I feel like in this little time and with my son's birthday, I have somehow come to make a complete circle.

Chapter 54
Tia Maria And Tio Juan
January 9, 1983

While helping with the Posadas, I got to know Tia Maria and Tio Juan's story. They have been married for over fifty-five years. They are both children of the original families who came to settle in La Laja. The families who settled here are no strangers to death, poverty, and hunger. I understand that these are Jose's family roots. His mother and father are also children of first-generation settlers. Both married in their teens and have 11 children, with only eight surviving.

Like most of his ancestors before him, Tio Juan lives off the land. He farms corn, beans, squash, and anything else that they eat in the household. Like him, he has taught his sons how to live off the land to feed their families. Like their parents and grandparents before them, they married very young and had many children.

Tio Juan and his brothers helped build what is now the surroundings of the six-house compound. Tio Juan's father and grandfather built the original one-room house that remains their home today. This home is where Tio Juan and later his children were born and grew up.

It is customary for a married couple that the husband brings his new bride to live with his family in his compound. The woman then becomes a daughter to her in-laws and a member of her husband's household. As a daughter (inlaw) she helps in the kitchen and house chores. Tio Juan was the first to marry in his family. As tradition calls it, he then brought Tia Maria (his wife) to live in his family home. Living here, they had seven children. Tio Juan, like his father, is a strong-mannered man. A hard-working farmer always ensures that his family, including his parents, is cared for. Tio Juan has learned to be a very responsible husband and successful farmer when nature permits it, just like his ancestors before him.

A few years into Tio Juan and Tia Maria's marriage, it was challenging to survive on your own. Nature was not kind, and rain was scarce. To top this off, by the 1940s the Mexican Revolution was over but it left many things unsettled in Mexico. The land reforms were made in the farmlands on the city's outskirts. Food became scarce because of the scarcity of rain. All these events contributed to some families moving out of the countryside and into the towns and cities to find, work.

One common way to feed the family was to cross the border into "El Norte" or the United States to find work. Tio Juan and his brother Tomas decided to venture out into the world of the *"El Norte"* in the United States. The word was that El Norte was the land of Opportunity. It offered fruitful job offerings in farms and fields, especially in California. This was very attractive for poor Mexican farmers.

Tio Juan worked a total of four years in American agricultural work before returning home. He was not pleased with his life in a foreign place. He missed his family and way of life, but leaving La Laja for those years gave way to his family's better life and survival.

Tia Maria held the family together during the time her husband was gone. She and their oldest son Manuel became head of the household and raised six younger children. These were hard times for everyone in La Laja and its surroundings. People did what they could to survive. This was also true for most Mexicans in the nation.

Tia Maria managed the little money she received from Tio Juan to make ends meet. While Tio Juan was away, they lost a Seven-year-old daughter due to a sort of pneumonia. Survival was hard at times, especially for young children. Although still a child himself, Manuel took his father's duties and quickly became an adult. The news of losing a child was devastating to the family.

It is even harder for Tio Juan because they were so far apart from each other. Tia Maria and Tio Juan dealt with this loss each on their own—one in Mexico and the other in the United States.

Tia Maria was not unfamiliar with death, for she lost two of her children in miscarriages. With only the help of a midwife and no medical professionals, there is a high number of miscarriages and newborn mortality in La Laja. For Tio Juan, living away in another country away from his family was very difficult. By his fourth year of being away, he decided to return to be with his family. This meant a modest life with very little money, but the family was together again. This experience taught Tio Juan and Tia Maria to appreciate family being together.

CHAPTER 55
DANCING LESSONS PART 2

Today the women woke up very excited and looking forward to their second day of dance class with me. They let me know last evening that they would be ready early. Today I will teach *"Folklorico"* A Mexican dance class that I often teach in Los Angeles. Regina, Elena, and their neighbor Socorro agreed to meet me on the patio where the class will take place. They hurried to finish their daily chores early, and are now free for the one-hour class.

"The men are in the fields working and the children are busy playing or at school," Socorro says. They told me that as children, and on special occasions, dancers from nearby towns would come to perform in the plaza. They confess that they always silently wished to be one of those dancers. They daydreamed about one day dancing like them. "The dancers wore pretty colorful dresses and ribbons on their hair." Regina said. "The children that were able to go to school in some of the villages had a chance to learn dances. But we didn't have teachers or school in La Laja at the time so no chance of ever dancing for us," Regina added. "Most of us didn't go to school and stayed at home to help our mothers and learn how to do chores and also take care of our younger siblings."

Rafaela and Marina are shy about saying anything about their childhood. They also feel that they are now too old to do such a thing as dance. They tell Regina this. "Nonsense," Tia Maria says. "I'm eighty-two years old but with the soul of a young girl, always wanting to escape this old and tired body to do the things I wanted to do as a child." "And one of these things is dancing!" "I believe that taking time for us is selfish. We have duties now." Rafaela says. "Our time has passed and now we must do what is destined to us by our age." Regina, Socorro, and Tia Maria disagree. "There is no correct or ideal age for dancing. It's in the spirit", Regina adds. Tia Maria immediately agrees.

A nice flat space on the patio is cleared and prepared for the lesson. Plants, *masetas,* and an eating table are all put to the side of the kitchen. I'm ready to begin. I ask the women to stand across me in a line and to follow me. Like me, I asked them to use their arms to simulate skirt movements. Again, Rafaela and Marina sit on the side and only observe. I could see the curiosity on their faces.

I now begin by demonstrating the first basic skirt movement. At first, the three ladies giggle and look at each other, trying to imitate my movements. I tell them to relax and think about our first lesson in the kitchen. Soon with much encouragement, they begin to take the lessons more seriously. They begin to follow me step by step. "One, two, three, Uno Dos Tres," I say loudly. I model the eight-figure symbol with my skirt. "Like ocean waves," I tell them. I repeat one, two, three repeatedly until the three begin to see and understand and finally follow.

Soon their movements are coordinated within themselves. Then I move on to footwork or steps. "One, two, three. Uno Dos Tres," I say and show them again, but this time with my feet. I indicate the difference between the left and right foot, thus beginning the basic step of *"zapateado."* This is their first difficult task, mainly because they are not wearing appropriate shoes. They have plastic sandals on, and moving with them is challenging. I remove my shoes and ask them to join me with a barefoot dance step. They do, and the dancing becomes more enjoyable and less difficult.

The three women persevere and, little by little, accomplish the coordination of hand and footwork. "I feel like I'm flying like a bird," says Socorro. Regina says that she wishes she had real dance shoes to make the sounds I make. After about an hour, the time for music came. *"El Son de La Negra "* is played on Manuel's record player. The women's eyes light up with excitement once they hear the music and as they follow their teacher. Regina and Socorro giggle like little children and say "Look at me, I can dance! I feel so happy Elena replies. "Felicidad "

I see from the corner of my eyes that during all this time, Rafaela and Marina have big smiles on their faces. I can tell that they, too, are enjoying the class even though they are not participating. I can see that they too, dance with their eyes and their smiles. It's like something inside them is magically being touched for the very first time. The dancers continue to follow me, and soon after a few minutes, they are able to dance on their own. This put a smile on my face. For more than an hour, we danced and enjoyed every minute. Soon I announce to them that the class is over for the day. It will continue tomorrow," I tell them.

All three women have put their heart and soul into every step of the dance. And they are now ready to clean up and put everything back in its place. I feel good about giving these women something back for all the good that they have given me.

CHAPTER 56
A VISIT FROM MARINA

FEBRUARY 8, 1982

After daybreak, when everyone had dinner and was relaxing from the hard day's work, I decided to walk alone out of the compound. I walk to my favorite place to be alone, a small hill overlooking the town plaza. I have been unexpectedly struggling this week with bad dreams and flashbacks. And I don't know why now? The memories came back and haunt me once more. Mental pictures of my son in his hospital bed with all the needles in his little arms and his head. I fight the image of seeing my child with a large needle plunged into his forehead. I remember the torture for my son and me that day so well.

It's been two days, and my thoughts are overwhelming, occurring even during the daytime. By now, the ladies notice that something is wrong. I'm quieter than usual, and they ask if I'm ok? I say, "I'm fine, and I need a little time to myself."

As I leave the compound, I stop by the shade of a large mango tree. By now, the memory of my son being tortured is even more clear in my mind. I could see him desperately trying to pull the needles and by moving his little head back and forth that he was fighting the needle in his forehead. His little hands are tied loosely to the bed frame like a little animal to prevent him from reaching his forehead. I could tell he was in a lot of discomfort and pain, but I couldn't do anything to help him. I begged the nurse to take the needle off his head, but she said it was all for his own good. The forehead was the only place they found a good vein to keep his IV and medications going.

In a few minutes, my son's crying was weak, breaking my heart. I cry in desperation and the nurse asks me to please leave the room. " How long is he going to have the needle in his head?" I ask before leaving. "Three more hours." She answers me. It is then that instead of cowardly leaving the room, I decide to compose myself, be strong for my son, and stay in the room with him. The least I could do for him is hold his little hand and tell him everything will be ok soon. This seemed to calm him somehow down, and eventually, he fell asleep little by little, holding my hand.

I don't know why this image came to my mind today. I don't know how or why but it's here with me digging at my soul. I came to sit in this place by myself where I can cry. I get up from sitting under the tree and climb a small hill. I found a spot where I can sit by a large rock overlooking the small plaza. It's a peaceful place here for me. I often come here to think about my family back home. I envision my husband and son being here with me, sitting on the rock, happily looking down at the plaza.

*After some time of sitting here alone, I hear some footsteps approaching me from the hill*side. I can tell that the person approaching me is being cautious. I slowly feel the steps closer and closer and finally, to my surprise, I can see that Marina is coming my way. I was shocked and very much surprised to see her. She is the last person I would expect to see looking for me.

Since arriving in La Laja, Marina and I haven't had any real personal conversations. There are no actual words between us. She is a resistant and private person and that's pretty much what I know about her. I know that after the tragedy of her children drowning, she has become a recluse, and pretty much keeping mostly to herself.

As Marina gets closer to me, and without saying a word, she very slowly and carefully comes and sits by my side. Placing her hand in my lap, she whispers, without ever looking at me *"Everything will get better."* "Crying is good for you and your soul," she tells me softly. "When crying becomes intense and very deep, it cleanses you." "That's what I have come to learn in all these years of mourning and pain," she explains. I listened to her words of wisdom and soon, I felt something heavy coming up through my heart and chest. I realize that it's something that's been hiding inside me for some time. A very deep and intense cry overwhelmingly came over me. I begin to cry. I cry so hard and loud that even the birds fly away in terror. Marina holds my hand to comfort me. Now Marina begins to cry with me. We are in communion with one another in this. In minutes our deep sobs become almost like one.

"I can't forget the visions," I tell Marina between sobs. "I can see my child with a large needle in his head, I see it over and over and can't get it to stop!" "I know that pain very well" Marina answers me, *this time looking at my face trying to look into my eyes.* "You will *never forget your son or* that vision, but it will get better with time" she assures me as she squeezes my hand.

"For many months and years, I couldn't fight off the vision of seeing my two young children desperately drowning in the river. I could still vividly see their desperation trying to float or hold on to a branch or something to keep them afloat. I could hear their cries calling me over and over while the harsh current of the water rolled their little bodies away. I could still feel the anxiety of being unable to reach my babies and save them from that terrible death. It is as if the devil himself chased me for days and nights with those horrific dreams and visions. *There were times when I wanted to throw myself onto the river and die, but I thought of my* remaining children and how they still need me."

"Through much praying and with time, little by little, I learned to face these dragons, each time with less pain and more understanding of what was going on in my head," she tells me. "In all my years of mental and emotional torture, I have finally come to find an answer. That answer is the *Blessed Mother Guadalupe.* I now know for a fact that women who lose children, like us, are **"chosen"** by angels and are blessed by God. I know that in my heart," Marina tells me this with great sincerity. " I believe that everything we go through in losing our children comes to be a privilege." We come to suffer as the blessed Mother did. To me, that's a privilege."

"Nuestra Madre Maria '', "witnessed all of her son's suffering. She saw the many beatings, whippings, spitting, and stoning by the people. Her son was savagely being stoned and poked by soldiers' spears. She saw the unworthy hate the people had for her son. She witnessed the torture of the beatings first hand, and eventually, she saw and felt his death by crucifixion at the foot of the cross."

"Because of The Blessed Mother and what she went through, I see her as my example of strength, acceptance, faith, and forgiveness. My faith has now become stronger than ever before. I now see the privilege of walking this journey as our Blessed Mother did."

I have come here to tell you that the Blessed Mother serves us as our role model for what we've gone and are going through." "She is always with us in our pain, comforting our soul and spirit." "She knows exactly what we feel and understands us completely.." We *are never alone in this short lifetime here in this lifetime." "We have the promise of seeing our children again in heaven." "I know I will see mine, and you will too,"* Marina tells me with such peace.

Marina continues, "I often think of Our Blessed Mother's story and come to realize that my experience in losing my children is painful and difficult to understand, but knowing the extent of her losing her adult son to human injustice is heartbreaking." "This lets me know that I am not and will never be alone in my grief and loss." That I am in the company of Mother Mary. "I have come here to this hill to let you know that."

Marina's passive wisdom impressed me. She is a quiet woman with a very knowledgeable spirit. Since my loss, nothing much has made any sense.

I don't know what to say now. In all my time here in La Laja, I never saw Marina in this light. She is a strong woman with great courage. I really admire her now for that. Marina then continues, "I must confess that it wasn't easy to realize." "It took much pain, tears, and suffering and at times great guilt before I was able to truly understand my journey." "The road has been hard, but with the words of a kind priest that spoke to me one day, I realized that our pain is the same as that of our Mother in Heaven."

"We are her children and she too suffers for us and with us. I know that I am not alone. The same goes for you too, and many other mothers who were chosen to take this journey with us. Good times and bad times will continue to come, but it will be better each time." In hearing Marina's words, I realize how strong Marina's faith has become. I see the freedom of pain and guilt on her face. I begin to think of the great lesson she has learned and that now she passes on to me. The one who never speaks has given me wise words and the greatest life lesson.

She has given me an explanation that I find logical and comforting. "I need to face the pain and let time heal me." I Think about how I have always loved the Blessed Mother and now that I know that she holds my hand with love and answers to my suffering." "Now I feel the love that the Blessed Mother has for both Marina and me, and other women like us. *"Bendita seas Madre Mia."*

Marina and I sit quietly on the rock, holding on to one another and looking down into the plaza. No other words need to be said now. I understand it all. We sit for hours looking at the sun going down, marking the end of a day, and the beginning of a new loving friendship. Thank you, Marina. **Gracias Madre Santa.**

CHAPTER 57
TALKING TO JOSE ON THE PHONE
FEBRUARY 12, 1983

By now going to the out house has become more accepting and even normal to me. By now I know what I needed to do to make sure that my visits to the outhouse are fearless and successful. I never thought I could do that. But I still ensure my visits occur before nightfall just in case. Jose laughs at me when I tell him this on the phone. I tell him, " I promise never to complain about the bathroom conditions back home."

As I get more and more comfortable here in La Laja, my phone calls home have become more frequent and more relaxed. In talking to Jose, he tells me that just by listening to me he can tell I'm making progress and doing much better here. "I can tell by the stories you share with me, especially the stories about the outhouse first visit and when you were trying to make tortillas and your acrylic nails caught on fire." Jose says with a bit of wit in his tone. I tell him about the dance lessons and how the women enjoy them. He tells me: "It sounds to me like you enjoy teaching more than they enjoy dancing." He knows me too well.

I also share with Jose some of the sad and tragic stories I have come to hear and witnessed here. Stories about women losing their children tragically. About the hardships that families have and about their relationships. " It sounds to me like you're making La Laja your second home," he tells me." "I'm so happy for you," he says. "Some of the stories here have broken my heart." I tell him about the old woman in the church. "Life gives happiness and tragedies," he says to me. "That's something that we know in life, it's inevitable." "The important thing is to have faith and believe that things will always be better with time," he tells me.

"That's what Tia Maria tells me," I tell him. "So far, the saddest story I've heard here is about Marina's children drowning in the River," I tell him. "Yes, I remember my cousin telling me that tragic story, the whole village was heartbroken and mourned the children along with the family." "I thought losing our son was tragic," I tell him, but now I realize there are far worse stories to tell.

"At least our son had a medical specialist working on his case and a hospital room and medicines to help him. I realize how lucky he was, that he was taken care of till his end, and how some of these children have very little"

I also tell him about sitting on the hillside with Marina, and what she shared with me. Jose tells me, "I'm glad Marina finally found her peace and that she is sharing it with you." "Your voice tells me you have made so much progress in your grief. I'm grateful to God for this." Jose now tells me he is ready to go to bed. " I have to work early tomorrow morning," he tells me. " Kiss Eddie for me," I tell him. He says, "I love you."

"I love you too," I said back to him as I hung up the

phone. I think I'm almost ready to return home.

CHAPTER 58
VALENTINES DAY AWAY FROM HOME

FEBRUARY 14, 1983

Today is Valentine's Day and I remember last year when Jose came to the hospital with flowers and we got to spend some time together with Xavier, as a family. Today I miss Jose dearly. It's Valentine's Day at home. I miss his hugs and his warm kisses. His kind words always tell me everything will be alright. This Valentine's Day is sad for me because Jose is so far away.

February 14, Valentine's Day, has no meaning here in La Laja. It is like any other ordinary day. I decided to get up and give everyone I see hugs and tell them that this is an American tradition called "Valentine's Day, a day of Love."

After I hugged almost everyone, they looked at me, wondering what was going on with me. Then brave Elena asked me, " Is February 14 the only day in America where you give hugs and love?" At first, I thought it was a silly question, but seeing Elena's genuine curiosity, I realized the truth about the question.

Tia Maria looks at me and says, "This thing about hugs and love is an everyday thing for us" she says. "We don't need a special day just for that, we do it all the time." And then she hugged me. I immediately felt her love and the love all around me. This is true, I say to myself, Valentine's Day is here every day. Happy Valentine's Day!

In the afternoon, I walked to the little store at the edge of the town to make a phone call home. Jose answered the phone with the words" "Happy Valentine's to My Valentine." I thanked him and said likewise. Then I told him about Elena's question, and he laughed. Then Eddie came to the phone and sang a little rehearsed

Valentine's song for me. This turned out to be a sweet Valentine's Day for me, after all.

CHAPTER 59
THE BITE

FEBRUARY 18, 1983

I woke up in the middle of the night sweating and with a high fever. I feel strong cramping in my stomach, nausea, and pain in my right arm. Struggling to sit up in bed, I somehow manage to call out Rafaela's name for help. She hears my call and quickly comes to my bed. I then see a look of deep concern on her face when she sees me.

Rafaela quickly tells me to lie down and to relax and that everything will be alright. Rafaela's youngest daughter comes in behind her and Rafaela instructs her to quickly call her grandmother Tia Maria for help. Tia Maria is sleeping nearby and she comes very quickly. She then notices my pale wet face which is very much in distress. She quickly instructs Rafaela "to go get some oil, water, and herbs from the kitchen, and to go get Socorro quickly."

Rafaela returns with the water and herbs that Tia Maria asked for and she and her daughter go to get Socorros who is also not far. Dona Maria quickly dips a white cloth in the water with yerba buena leaves and places it on my forehead until Socorro arrives. Socorro arrives with her basket of herbs and quickly takes a look at my right arm which I complain about the pain and which by now is very swollen.

Socorro tells me to take long deep breaths and not to panic. I began to tremble in shock as if I was very cold. I soon begin to hallucinate and start calling Jose who I see sitting in the corner of the room, holding our young sons Eddie and Xavier. I raise my arms towards them and ask them to come closer. Tia Maria then notices a sort of bite in the upper part of My right arm as I stretch it. it's a scorpion bite she says an *"alacran"* bit her!

The women get to work quickly to stop the spread of poison. "Scorpions and bites are common but at times deadly this time of year," Socorro tells Tia Maria as she looks at my arm to confirm it. Regina quickly enters the room with a special serum made of different wild herbs for scorpion bites: "We must move quickly before the venom reaches her heart." Regina adds.

My body has begun to stiffen, and my hallucinations continue to strengthen now. I now see my mother and sisters bringing me a white gown and telling me to "get dressed. We are taking you back home with us." Wet with fever, I get up and say, "It's time for me to go home now." The three women somehow manage to take me back to my bed. "We must give her the serum to drink now!" Socorro says, "I have the serum." The serum is in a tube-like bamboo dispenser, and as the two women hold me down on the bed, Socorro places the tube in my mouth and quickly empties it down my throat.

Then they immediately changed my wet clothes to dry ones. Dona Maria begins to pray with great concern to the Blessed Mother. "We need to put these wet herbs around her body until the fever cuts," Socorro explains, especially around the arm close to the heart.

By this time, the men have gathered outside the patio to see what they can do to help. Tio Juan tells Manuel to have the truck ready in case they need to take me quickly to the nearest medical center. The men are concerned with their promise to Jose to take care of his wife. And as usual in such circumstances, they stand ready to help in any way they can.

Regina begins to clear the air in the room by burning incense and placing it between two white candles. Marina starts to pray with Dona Maria. Elena brings in a clay pot with special tea for me to drink. "We must help her clean her system," Socorro says as she helps me sit upward on a stack of pillows. "Drink this tea," she says as she puts the tea between my lips to sip.

At first, I was too stiff and found it very difficult to follow her directions. "Drink your tea." Elena tells me kindly as she approaches the opposite side of the bed to hold my hand. "Your body needs to flush out the scorpion's poison." My high and persistent fever is scaring all the women, and soon I begin to have small convulsions. "Blessed Mother, help her!" Tia Maria prays when she sees me convulsing. "She's very sick now. Marina quickly tells Socorro: "Hurry, give her some more tea". To get me to drink more tea Marina sits me up in the bed with pillows. I open my eyes and call "Little Gabriel's" name. "Are you here to get me home, little Gabriel?" I say. "Why are you floating on top of my bed?" I ask him.

The women have no idea of what I'm saying or who I'm talking to. "Gabriel, little Gabriel, I miss you," I tell him as I look above at the wooden ceiling, and the women know now that I'm hallucinating.. "You're going to be alright, " Gabriel tells me softly, angelically. "You're going to live for your children." Still, in my trance, Gabriel gives me his little hands, and I put them next to my heart. Then he kisses my forehead and suddenly he's gone. I slowly take a sip of tea, then again. One more sip and then I lay down in bed. Seeing my peaceful smile, Tia Maria says, "an Angel has come to save her."

Hours later the whole compound is still worried. Soon the night is over, and it begins to be daybreak. By now the women are sleeping in chairs around me. Socorro wakes up and reaches out to touch me, and notices that the fever finally broke. "The fever is gone!" Socorro says, quickly waking up the other ladies. "She's going to be fine!" The women thanked God and the Blessed Mother and rejoiced with happiness. It is a miracle, Tia Maria says, the bite was severe. The men are told the happy news, and soon the patio is filled with a grateful family.

The women decide to make the morning meal for the men and children, while Tia Maria stays with me while I still sleep. A few minutes later I begin to slowly wake to the beautiful morning brought to my room, through the window. "What happened?" I ask Tia Maria. "You were bitten by a scorpion sometime last evening and you were very sick." "I feel so sore and very tired," I say, and then I noticed my arm is very swollen. "Why does my arm hurt so much when I move it?" "You had a high fever," Tia Maria tells me. A scorpion bite does that, and it makes you delusional, that is why you don't remember anything." "I remember one thing," I said to her. "What do you remember?" Does Tia Maria ask? "I remember holding Little Gabriel in my arms." "Is that your little son?" "No, Gabriel is a little boy who I met in the hospital and who died before my son died." "I grew very fond of this little boy and loved him and took care of him as much as I could." "And he came to take care of you last night, no doubt about that" Tia Maria tells me. "Really?" I ask her. "Yes," she says "He is one of your guardian angels."

CHAPTER 60
THE LETTER

Then the end of February came, and no Valentine's letter for Elena from Santiago as she had received before and now expected. Elena looks forward to receiving a letter from her fiance Santiago once a month as usual. By now, Santiago has been in the United States for almost two years. She is in love with her childhood sweetheart and hopes and prays for his fast return.

At first, his letters were very constant, telling her how much he misses her and that he can't wait to make enough money and return to marry her. He has been sending money to buy cement and *"ladrillo"* blocks to start building their small two-room house.

Elena always daydreams about the kind of little house they will build for themselves once they marry.

Elena even has her wedding dress made just as she dreamed of. Her brother promised her a big fiesta celebration, complete with the killing of two pigs and a goat for food for the celebration. Everything is all set for the wedding, and everyone is looking forward to and anticipating the wedding to take place soon.

It's been three months since Elena received the last letter from Santiago. All letters and calls have stopped. At first, Elena is afraid that something might have happened to Santiago. His cousin Martin calls his wife from the U.S. to La Laja every week. He lives near Santiago and he confirms that Santiago is fine. Elena wonders why he hasn't responded to any of her letters. Elene is beginning to feel terrified that he has forgotten her.

The news spreads quickly in the village that Santiago might have another girlfriend in the U.S. Elena doesn't want to listen to gossip or stories about men who have left their girlfriends in the villages to marry another woman in El Norte. Elena refuses to give up on the promises Santiago made to her. "He couldn't have stopped loving me," she tells herself. Again two months go by, and again no letters from Santiago to Elena.

One day Elena finally receives a letter from her love. Before even opening the letter, Elena jumps for joy and goes and shares the good news with her family. "Open the letter," they say! "What does he say, is he coming soon?" Elena is nervously shaking her hands but manages to open the letter quickly. She starts with a bright smile on her face but very soon the smile begins to fade. Elena continues reading, and soon her eyes stop shining and her enthusiasm fades. "Que pasa?" "What does the letter say?" Tio Juan asks, "Is Santiago alright?" Manuel asks.

But Elena could not answer. Her hands tremble even more. She seems frozen in time and doesn't respond to any questions. With a blank stare, Elena drops the letter on the floor. Her father, Tio Juan, bends down and picks up the letter, and begins to read it. His face falls with disgust, *"Poco Hombre"* he says as he crumples the letter and throws it to the ground once more. *"Que pasa?"* Tia Maria asks with great concern. "Did something happen to Santiago?" "I wish it did!" Tio Juan screams out as he walks out the door and exits. "I'm going to see Santiago's parents right now so they can explain all this he says!" He then gets on his horse and rides it away.

"He's marrying someone else," Elene quietly utters the words out of her mouth. "He is not coming back to marry me! He loves somebody else." "But what about the promises he made to you?" Her mother asks. "There are no real promises, they were all lies," Elena says and falls into a rage of tears. Her cries are heard by the women of the compound and they soon come to her side, and find out the contents of the letter. The women try to console Elena, but there are no words or actions for such terrible news. Elena has broken. *"me quiero morir"* "I want to die!" Elena cries out to the world, as her mother comes to her side and embraces her in her arms. Tia Maria is also in tears and feels helpless in trying to help ease her daughter's pain.

Tio Juan rides his horse to Santiago's parent's house to demand that their son do good to his promise to his daughter. "There is nothing we can do to help your daughter," they say. Santiago's parents come out to meet him at their patio. They are very ashamed and apologetic about their son's actions towards Elena and the family. They too, don't seem to understand why their son is doing such a terrible thing. And there is not much they can do to change the situation. "We are told by family members living there that he is now getting married to someone else ". "He tells us that the woman he is marrying has promised to fix his immigration papers once he marries her." "I'm so sorry, Juan " Santiago's father says, really meaning it. We have been good friends since childhood. I'm so sorry my son is doing this to Elena and your family, it's very shameful. I know my son still loves Elena, but his ambition of wanting to be legal in El Norte has overtaken him"

"Your son Santiago is willing to lose my daughter Elena for immigration papers '? "Then he never really loved her." I tell you now that this news is not only breaking my daughter's heart but the whole family's heart too." "We will never forgive him for this." Now my daughter is condemned to live with this shame forever"!

It has been two weeks since the letter arrived in Elena's hands. By now she has fallen into a deep depression and now refuses to leave the house. She is ashamed of being seen left at the altar. **"Vestida y alborotada"** Left at the altar is worse than death in a place like La Laja. Elena is sure that no other man will ever look at her again and she will always be known as the old maid left behind by Santiago. Her parents are very worried about her. They don't know what to say or do to help. Word has come that Santiago is now married to an *"American Woman"* and that he has moved away to another state far from his friends and cousins.

I decided to visit Elena and try to talk to her and convince her that things will pass. "You are a beautiful young girl, with a future life ahead of you," I tell her. She reminds me that in La Laja, the only thing a girl can look forward to is getting married and having children. "Nothing else exists for us here." "We are raised from a very young to take care of children, keep the house clean, and learn to cook. That is our schooling, she says, and our reality." And there are no real eligible young men available to marry since most couples here marry very young."

"I have no real future," she says sadly. At this point, I feel so helpless with Elena. I don't know what else to say or do to help her feel better. I realize that we come from two different worlds and it's hard in this situation,

Elena is not talking or eating much. She tells me that "Santiiago's betrayal makes her feel worthless." How can I possibly have her understand, or convince her that this is not true? What can I say or do to make her want to live again, like the happy girl I met when I first came here? In my feeling of helplessness, my frustration comes in, but I must not go too deep into it, for I have made much progress in my personal life so far. I have been in a state of depression and not believing in myself. "I can't just step aside and let her destroy herself like this." " It's all so familiar." I ask myself. "Where is her faith?" "The one Tia Maria speaks of all the time?" "I wonder now?"

Weeks have gone by and I decide to go to see Tia Maria concerning her daughter Elena. I ask her what could be done to help her. *"Let God and let time, "* she answers me calmly. Somehow I get upset at the way she candidly carries herself when it comes to talking about her youngest daughter's situation. I now know that I need to be patient and respectful of their beliefs and ways that the people here have.

"Something good will come to Elena, from all this," Tia Maria says. "She is very young and God has other plans for her other than Santiago." I am amazed by the serenity in her words. "We just need to wait and see what God has for her now." By now I have no choice but to believe in what she says. I will do my best to understand it all. I know I will be leaving La Laja soon, and I don't want to leave Elena like this. "Be Patient, belief, and trust," Tia Maria tells me. "God has better plans for Elena." "Remember that everything in this life happens for a better reason." "God knows our hearts and loves us." "No matter how deep the pain and dissolution is, it will all pass." "I trust my Lord," she says, looking at me with a smile on her face, she says: "You should too."

Chapter 61
Good News About Teaching
March 29, 1983

Time goes by, and Elena slowly recovers from her broken heart. She begins her healing by being with the children, which she loves. The children somehow bring her back to life, she says. One day La Laja gets news from Guadalajara about someone coming from the Department of Education with the duty to train people who may be interested in teaching in their villages. Elena, having always enjoyed being around children and teaching young ones, is encouraged by her mother and everyone else to attend the training. Tia Maria hopes this opportunity will help her forget her situation with the canceled wedding.

Most of the villages in the area are in dire need of teachers. Again Elena is encouraged by the whole family and village to take advantage of this once-in-a-lifetime opportunity. Elena now sees the opportunity she always dreamed of, so she joins the group in training. Elena is the only female of the eight that signed up for the training.

The training begins with introducing Professor Roberto Ruiz, a young but very formal and intelligent instructor with many expectations for the group. He is sent from Guadalajara hoping to start very much-needed school teachers and schools in this area.

Professor Ruiz is a nice-looking young man in his late twenties who is being hosted for the next two months or eight weeks by the church priest in La Laja. The Professor will be staying to train future teachers. Once the group begins, he comes to find out that Elena is the only female in the group. Elena is immediately overtaken by the professor's good looks and evident intelligence, which she admires. She has never met a man like him before.

Elena never misses a moment in her training and learning. She reads all that the Professor requires of her, and the professor is always complimenting her on her eagerness to learn quickly. "I've always wanted to be a teacher," she tells him. And he answers, "I can tell." He is very impressed by Elena's natural passion for teaching. This is something that they both have in common. Elena and the professor spend many days and hours together working side by side, and by doing this, in a short time, she seems to have forgotten Santiago.

Weeks and days pass, and by the eighth week the group is finally done with the training. Elena is finally and officially a certified teacher. She is immediately then given a small group of kids in La Laja to teach. Elena can't believe her luck. She thanks God for this blessing. She can't believe everything that has happened to her in such a short time. Her life has made changes for the best. Now she feels she has everything she ever wanted, to be a teacher. And she now has a life to look forward to.

"God is good," Tia Maria tells her daughter. Elena soon begins to teach her little group, beginning with Dona Tomasa's grandchildren who are so eager to attend school. Her group comes together quickly and the state of Jalisco promises to build a three-room school for her very shortly. The village also comes to celebrate this great success of finally having a school and having Elena as their teacher.

When the professor's work is finally complete, it is time for him to return to Guadalajara. Elena is sad to see him go, she will miss him, and it seems that the professor feels the same way too. With Elena and Mr. Ruiz spending so much time together, the inevitable has occurred, they fall madly in love with one another. After losing Santiago, Elena believed she would never be happy or fall in love again. But she was wrong, here she is now, in love with Roberto and becoming a teacher.

The Professor said, "he must return to Guadalajara, but promises Elena he will return for her and ask her hand in marriage." Elena has heard this promise before with Santiago and tells herself to take Roberto's promise lightly. The professor doesn't write to Elena; instead, he calls her from Guadalajara to the corner store telephone every other day on the dot. Elena has not told anybody about Roberto's promise to return to marry her. She doesn't want to go through with the ridicule she lived with Santiago. Instead, she concentrates on her job and thanks God every day for such a blessing. Now no matter what happens in her life, she will be content in her passion.

Several weeks go by, and Roberto announces his arrival to Elena. He says he loves her and misses her so much and that he's returning to La Laja to marry her. In a matter of two weeks after this announcement, Elena and Roberto are finally ready to marry in the little plaza church. Their wedding is simple but beautiful and Elena finally wears her beautiful wedding dress. She looks so beautiful, just like a princess, her father says. Everyone in the village attends the wedding and is very happy for the couple. Elena's patience and belief have paid off well. "She will make a wife and a good teacher" Rafaela and the women say. Professor Roberto is a man who not only has come to love Elena but also admires her as a woman.

Tia Maria cries at the wedding. Her tears are that of joy and happiness for her daughter. Tia Maria never lost faith in God's best plan for her daughter. In time, Elena and the professor plan to open a small school in La Laja, not only for children but also for adolescents and adults who want to learn how to read or sign their names. This is very needed in the village. The village is grateful for this, for most of the adults never had a chance to go to school. Elena feels proud to be Roberto's wife and now sees herself someday having her own children to care for.

In a few weeks, I'll be going back home to Los Angeles, and Elena's story, like many other stories here, has also taught me a valuable life lesson. We may not understand right away why some losses or tragedies occur in our lives. But if we are patient, believe, and trust in God, those hurtful events eventually bring or return something good or better to our lives. This was most definitely the case with Elena. Her patience and beliefs were rewarded for the better. And I believe so will mine.

CHAPTER 62
CHILDHOOD "MUNECAS"
CHILDHOOD MEMORIES

APRIL 3, 1983

Before I leave La Laja, the women ask me about "my counseling job and what I do with this?". I tell them that "I do many things, like talk to people about their problems and have helpful workshops." "Workshops they ask?" "Yes," I answered them. This is when "I work with a group and talk and sometimes play grown-up games." Can you do that with us?" They quickly ask me. "Can we play a game like you say?" "We can. Still, in order to make this game a success, I need a quiet inside room for two hours." "I also need for you to have no distractions or interruptions from anybody for those two hours. For you to take what I say seriously, and trust me." "We can arrange for that,"

Regina quickly says. "Si, of course, we could, we trust you!" They quickly agreed. "We can do this when the men go to work. The children are given a job and told to stay away for two hours." "Can we play your game tomorrow"? Elena asks with excitement? "Yes, we can, I tell them, but again, you all need to take this game very seriously." "We will do as you say," answers Rafaela.

The next day, the women get up earlier than usual to make breakfast and prepare the mid-day meal. The men knew nothing about what was about to happen. They just wondered why the women were so secretive and so excited. As soon as the men left to work in the fields, and the children tended to their tasks, the women were ready to begin.

We decided that the workshop would take place in Rafaela's long front room. This was a perfect place because it is the largest room in the compound, and the windows in the room have dark curtains. The dark curtains are needed to be able to get the room dark enough for the women to concentrate.

I begin by having the chairs set in a circle around the room. Tia Maria decided to join the group and she brought her sister Christina, another older woman from the village, to join us. Tia Maria told me, "sister needs to play the game," "Whatever the game was?" Then I find out that Christina suffers from depression and Tia Maria wants to help her. I was happy that they trusted me. I welcome Christina to the group session.

I begin the session by closing the windows, door, and curtains. All this is to avoid all distractions or interrupting from the outside. I tell them that "no matter how different or funny my instructions are, they need to follow them exactly as they are told and take them very seriously if they want a good outcome in the game."

I then instruct them to " close their eyes and take deep breaths." All the women have a hard time doing this first task because it is all so new and unfamiliar to them. I then model the breathing for them and ask them to imitate by telling them to "take deep breaths in through the nose and to breathe out through the mouth." The giggling soon begins and starts to overtake them, but I remind them that "not taking each step seriously will prevent me from playing and completing the game with them."

They all agree to settle their nerves and cooperate with me. After the breathing is somewhat established, I tell them to "close their eyes and visualize a beautiful green forest." This is so they can learn to use their minds to see and to be able to concentrate on what they are seeing. The second thing I asked them to "visualize is a waterfall with a full running stream falling down a mountainside." I asked them to "hear the water roaring and falling on rocks and to feel the fresh breeze from the water on their faces." The third thing I ask them to "visualize is their childhood home." This is where things began to get serious.

I ask them to "visualize a day in their childhood house." I tell them to "carefully see it, the door and windows and things around them, their bed, the kitchen, the dishes on the table and what they were wearing?" I can soon tell by their faces that they successfully traveled back in time. I have now spent time with them exploring with their minds what their homes and surroundings were like. I tell them that "they are back in time for that special day. And to feel what that day felt like."

Now it is time to take them for instance to find a childhood memory. I take them to a place or time when they were children and loved to play. I help them by telling them to "look back at what toys made them happy as children." I also ask them to "look at what they are wearing and how they feel." I tell them to "go through the physical motions of playing." I tell them that "they can also sing or talk if they feel they should." My heart jumps when their faces go from adults to children after a while. Still with their eyes closed, their smiles are radiant and seem very curious. By this time, I am the one filled with full emotions.

By now, I am being transported into the world of childhood memories. I now witness the women simulating their memory experience by singing children's songs. Some are speaking to their dolls and/or serving food with their little clay dishes. I am able to see the little girls emerging from being deeply hiding inside these women's souls. Even Tia Maria and her sister Christina, being the elders in the group, seem to also be deep into their childhood memories and visions. I'm now witnessing a playground of happy children.

I now tell them that "they are allowed to stand up, dance or walk if they wish to. But they are to always keep their eyes closed and in the vision." The room soon became one of the most beautiful and touching scenes. One I have never witnessed in my lifetime. Two little girls danced, one singing and one talking to her doll. I can now see and feel their freedom and happiness in their childhood memories. After a few minutes of this heavenly celebration, I slowly instruct them to "sit down to relax and to bring their memory back with them." Step by step, I slowly regress their memory and concentration to the present. And now I tell them to "slowly open their eyes and be ready to share their experiences with one another.

The women began to open their eyes slowly, and without saying a word, they began to look at one another and around the room. Once the curtains are slightly opened, I ask them to "take more deep breaths and be ready to speak and share their memories with each other one at a time." At first, the women were hesitant to share or even speak, but I assured them that everything said in the room was considered safe and confidential. After that, they all promised not to share the stories with other people but themselves, then they slowly began to share.

Socorro Is the first to begin to share her memory. Her vision was about her corn husk doll that her grandfather very lovingly made for her, and which she named Margarita, like the flowers that grow wild in the mountains. "My grandfather glued small black seeds on the doll's face as eyes and mouth." These words brought Socorro to tears. She begins to share, "My grandfather, who was almost blind, made me this doll with lots of love. He tore out a piece of his old shirt he was wearing to make a little tunic for Margarita to wear." "My grandfather always did anything and everything possible to make me happy. "When my grandfather made the tunic for my doll, this inspired me to sew and make things by hand." "I eventually made dresses for Margarita and other dolls too." "I love my grandfather and even though he's been gone for years, I saw him alive in my vision." Socorro cries again. "He was so real. I hugged him and I was able to smell his clothes and hear his sweet voice again." My love for sewing came from seeing my grandfather caring about my doll." "And I have never forgotten this," she says in tears. With Socorro's beautiful and touching memoir, many of us feel the sentiment and cry.

Now **Tia Maria** has decided to share her vision. "My memory took me back to when my sisters and I made little dishes from mud piles to play. I remember happily playing with my little mud dishes, even though the dishes never lasted very long. They dried up and eventually cracked and crumbled." Tia Maria begins to cry. "My other memory is of going with her mother to clean the farm owner's large house, where I saw his little daughter sitting in the living room playing with real small plastic and porcelain dishes." "I had never seen such beautiful dishes, so much that I couldn't keep my eyes off of them. They were so beautiful." "My mother quickly scolded me and told me that we were there to clean that house and not to stare at toys." "I could also see the sadness in my mother's eyes for not being able to buy me any real toys." Tia Maria's young voice began to crack and cry. "All I wanted was to look at the toys, not touch them," she said.

After cleaning the house and as we were leaving, I saw the owner's daughter again, but this time she was holding a beautiful blond doll with pretty blue eyes in her arms. The doll had a beautiful blue dress and a white apron. She had a beautiful large shiny blue bow on her head. When my mother saw that I was fascinated looking at this, she quickly took me by the hand out of the house and we never spoke about this again.

Even though I thought I had forgotten it, this memory came back today. In this exercise, I was able to return to that house and time and finally hold that blonde doll in my arms and cradle her to sleep. "What a beautiful memory I have," Tia Maria says. She thanks me with tears of gratitude and says, thank you for taking me back there again. "Now I was able to hold that beautiful doll in my arms."

But not all memories are happy. Tia Maria's sister **Christina** begins to sob with her sister's story, and I quickly notice something I had not noticed since she got to the room. Like hiding something, Chistina carefully kept her right hand inside her apron pocket. I soon realized, when she suddenly and unintentionally pulled out her hand out of her pocket, that she was missing her right hand.

My initial reaction was shocking to see! But I did not say or do anything about it, so as not to put her in any shame or discomfort. Christina said she had "a very sad memory to share with us, instead of a happy one." I told her, "I respected that, and those memories are important too." I soon realized, by their reactions, that some of the women already knew the story behind how she came to lose her hand in her childhood.

Christina tells her memory: "When I was seven years old, my mother and I waited late one night for my father to arrive home from the plaza. I remember that it was a Friday and my mother and I prayed the rosary. It was pretty late when my father got home and he was very drunk."

"He began to yell at my mother for no reason. He pushed and began kicking her on the floor. I began to beg my father to stop, and he pushed me down to the floor too. He kept kicking my mother as she tried to protect her head from his beatings. My mother yelled at me to run and go get help, but I could not leave my mother alone. I could not decide what to do.

"Suddenly, I saw my father pulling out his *"machete"* from its case and pointing it to my mother, ready to attack her. I frantically ran in front of my mother and put my right hand up to protect her, when all of a sudden, my father, in an uncontrollable raging move, waved the machete and sliced my hand off my arm."

"Both my mother and my father fell in shock as they saw my blood gushing out of my arm. My mother began screaming, wailing, and calling for help! Quickly my mother gathered all her strength to get up from the now very bloody floor, to pull the tablecloth from the kitchen table somehow to quickly wrap it around my bleeding arm."

"My father ran out of the house screaming in terror, asking God for forgiveness. I'm not sure why this memory came to me today. I guess because after this day I never really played with anyone or did anything with children anymore. Not even my corn husk doll that I loved, gave me back the child joy I had before this happened."

By now I could not contain my emotions with Christina's story. It is too overwhelming for me or anybody else in the room. With no dry eye in the room, I quickly realized that this exercise helped Christina bring out her deep memory of this terrible event to finally share it with us. After a good cry, Christina continued, "I guess that deep inside me I have always wanted to play with my corn husk doll." " I now realize that I always wanted to but was ashamed of my hand."

The room is quiet with total silence, tears in everyone's eyes. An air of love, compassion, and love for Christina overflowed the room for a few minutes. By this time I was worried that maybe I had opened a whole new can of worms and wondered if I could really help these women.

Even though I have done this exercise many times before, I feel that this is a new experience for me to handle. I now ask my Lord for guidance in helping these women and their situations.

Regina now begins to share. "I have a happy story," she says "to break the ice." "My memory takes me back to when I used to play with my cousins on the river bank. After swimming we would go to the wet sand and soil and make different animal figurines. Then we would pretend to be at the farmhouse with our little cows, horses, goats, cats, and dogs. We would spend hours happily playing like this until it was time to go home."

"I always miss not having a real doll. My mother kept having babies and I was the oldest, so I had to help care for them. I always pretended that my little infant brothers and sisters were my dolls and that I was the mommy to play with and care for. It was fun, but at the same time, it was a lot of work for a little girl like me." "Especially when they cried or were sick or got too heavy for me to carry. The worst was getting them off their diapers and getting them to squat to poop." Everyone laughs at what Regina says. "I never got a real doll. My only doll was made of straw, but sooner or later, my little sisters would take it from me to play with. And since they were younger, I let them. I'm so happy to have this memory back.

Rafaela now decides to tell her story. She says, "every year after the corn harvest she would get a new corn husk doll which her mother made and dressed with whatever rags she could find." "After a while, I had a whole collection of corn husk dolls. I had a mother, grandmother, children, and even the father doll. I had so much fun playing with my little pretend family."

"One day my mother decided that at the age of seven, I was getting too old to play with dolls and she decided to hide them from me. My mother explained that her mother took her dolls away at seven too." "And that is when my house chores began. " My mother told me that I was wasting too much playing instead of helping her in the kitchen."

" My heart was broken." Rafaela continues: "I missed my little pretend family terribly. I remember secretly searching for my straw dolls everywhere and whenever I had a chance to do so. I looked in places I thought I could find them, but I was always unsuccessful. One day, while cleaning the kitchen, I looked behind the wood stove and found them! I was so happy to see them. Looking at them, I soon realized that most of them were half burned from the heat and sitting under the wooden stove."

"When I finally dared to show them to my mother, she told me I had to grow up and be a strong young lady. Life will be hard, and losses will come, and I will soon be a woman and will experience this." She said, "You need to learn this to survive in life."

Her words made my heart feel heavy, and I was unsure what she meant. All I knew was that my doll family was half burned and that I missed playing with them. My mother looked at me and saw my sadness. She then looked straight into my face and said, *"Women suffer all the time, and you need to know this now."* By now I am even more confused. I know that my mother had me when she was only fourteen and she never really had a childhood.

"A few days later my mother surprised me. She made a bigger straw doll for me." She said that "This doll was mine when I was seven, just like you." "And I was able to play with her only when all my chores were done." "This made me so happy, I could not believe that my mother did such a thing for me." "I spent most of my free time playing with my doll which I named Clementina. I always placed Clementina next to my bed at night before going to sleep."

"In time. My house duties grew and I had less time to play with my Clementina." "Now grown up and married at 17, I still have my Clementina doll under my mattress to look at when Munuel is not around to see me." "This doll is the only thing I have left from my mother, and is the only thing I brought here from my village."

Today's memory makes me feel that it's ok to be my age and still have my straw doll with me. When I hold her, I make sure nobody is around. Holding Clementina gives me so much comfort and love. I will always be seven years old when I hold her.

Marina decides not to share her vision. She says she had nothing to share from her childhood. " I had no dolls or toys," she says. "Most of my time was spent cutting flowers and leaves to make little houses for the ants and grasshoppers." "That's all I have to say." Marina's face seems saddened and I feel in my heart that there was more to her memory than what she shared with us.

Elena decides now to tell her story from the youngest child in the group's point of view. " I had a happy childhood. One day my father went to see a doctor in the city and came home with a plastic doll for me. All the girls wanted to see and hold my doll. They told me I was so lucky to get a doll like that. I named my doll Martita after the first and only teacher I had in my only three years of schooling."

"Martita's legs didn't fold so she could not sit when I played school with her and only lay down in a small straw bed I made for her ''. "She had black curly hair and her lips were red, and she made a good student." "I still have Martita in my *"Ropero" armoire.* And plan to one day give it to my daughter.

Unlike Christina's sharing, at this time now the room is gleaming with smiles that seem to understand and share a mutual childhood sentiment. And now they say "It's my turn to share one of my childhood memories with them." They ask me what my childhood was like living in America.

I begin by telling them that first, it was very hard for me, at the age of seven, to leave my home and half my family in Mexico." At That particular time, America was not speaking Spanish and there was no bilingual education. That meant that no one at school spoke

Spanish, not even the teachers." "This meant that I really just had to learn to survive on my own, and so I lived in my little world." "I started school in the second grade, and all the students made fun of how I dressed and combed my hair. It was a whole different way of living there." "Not knowing what they were saying, I had to learn to ignore their unkind words and actions, especially what I believed were humiliations." "With no friends or anybody speaking Spanish, I felt there was nothing I could do about my problems at school.."

"I quickly found refuge on our first Christmas in America. My sister and I each got a beautiful blonde doll from Santa Claus. We loved our beautiful dolls and always played house in the backyard with them."

"I remember making our dolls their furniture from empty cornflakes boxes, paper grocery bags, and paper towels for clothes and blankets. "My father and mother always made sure we played and had a good childhood experience." "Sometimes, the neighbors would give us the toys their children didn't want anymore, and we were happy with that. Except for the fact that I was miserable at school, my childhood memory with my doll and toys was a pleasant one." I finished telling them.

We finally concluded the session on childhood memories. I now remind the women of honoring each other's privacy once we begin to get ready to leave the room, but before doing so, I then ask them for their final comments. They all said that they enjoyed the memory and most of all they enjoyed the sharing time. "We never share things like this," Regina says. "It was nice to do so."

At the end of the session, the women were all eager to talk and share with one another at a later time on their own. I thank them for trusting me with their beautiful stories. "Now we have a connection with you," they say with a smile on their faces. Even Marina and Rafaela smile at this, making me feel and believe that my story and our conversations have somehow also made a difference in their childhood memories and their lives.

Chapter 63
Living in La Laja
May 1,1983

"Living in La Laja for all these months has made a great impression on me and changed my life so far in many ways forever. I find that the life stories here are really like so many anywhere on the planet." "We are all like a large mountain of sand, all together and all the same."

What I'm learning in this journey is that what *matters most is not what happens to you, but how you deal with what happens to you.* "Life gives us many things to deal with in our journeys that eventually, whether we are aware or not, take us to the place we are supposed to be to find our answers." Through all the stories I learned here in La Laja, especially the women's stories, I have come to realize many things about myself, one being how I handled my life circumstances in the past.

It's getting to be time for me to finally return home with all my gifts. The extraordinary thing is that I feel that La Laja is also my home now. I now feel a strong connection with people, especially the women. Living here all these months has made a great impression in my life. I find that the life stories I came across here are really all alike in so many ways. Wherever you go or in whatever place you live, life and death happen. I'm coming to learn that, I now know that what matters is how one comes to deal with the situation.

CHAPTER 64
TIME TO RETURN HOME

MAY 03, 1983

It's time to return to Los Angeles. Fernando and his wife Laura came to pick me up early Saturday morning. They are here to take me back to Guadalajara's airport. It's time to fly back home. I'm excited yet saddened to leave this place. In speaking on the phone with Jose last night, he told me how Eddie and he are anxious to see me, and to finally have me home. After all these months of being away from home, I feel happy to finally be returning to my little family again.

Leaving La Laja feels like leaving my second home. This place and its people have given me so much. Jose was right about learning so many lessons in this place, and finding myself in my spirit here. Everyone from Rafaela to Regina to Socorro Marina, Elena, Tia Maria,

Christina, and all the other women, have taught me life lessons. One of the most important lessons is how to face tragedy. I fell in love with people's energy in wanting to continue living no matter how heavy their burden was/is. I admire their passion for the little things in life and for to continue living.

I learned how to be completely free by just looking at their freedom. I felt their love. I never felt alone here and was always taken care of. The night I got sick, and how they took care of me were prime examples of their love for me and other human beings, and this I will never forget as long as I live. During the time spent here, I felt all along taken care of by a giant mother or, (all women together).

Now that it's time for me to leave, a piece of my heart stays here, and this is precisely where a new ME is born. I can see the sadness in everyone's eyes for my departure. I have grown close to all the children, men and women but especially Rafaela and Marina whose quiet spirit showed me that the child inside them and all of us are still living and never die.

When the women danced I saw the freedom that music and song can bring to people. I saw and learned the knowledge of the mountains and the beauty of the creeks and their gifts to mankind. I saw the children's faces filled with hope and joy with little things, and the elderly people with wisdom gave me peace. I saw the best in the simple things in life and I know it's all around if we just take the time to see. One of the most important things I learned here is that family is number one, whether blood-related or not. I feel I have found my new mother and sisters here.

As always, the women make a very special feast for my farewell breakfast. It's complete with the most delicious food, beautiful dishes, and colorful tablecloths. The children bring flowers and little mud figurines toys for me to take back home to Eddie. Rafaela knitted a special blanket to take back home. Tamales and tortillas were specially made to take home to Jose.

Breakfast is as wonderful as ever. The table setting and food look and smell so delightful. I'm sad to think that I'm leaving. Some women have teary eyes, especially Tia Maria and Marina. They say they are sad to see me leave and that they will miss me. This touches me. I tell them that I will miss them too, as we have a warm embrace.

The men said their goodbyes to me last night, for they would be leaving pretty early in the morning for the fields. Tio Juan, a modest man, in tears, tells me he loves Jose like a son and wants him to come to visit. He also tells me to give a message to Domitila, my mother-in-law, and his sister. He says he misses her and loves her very much. And that he is eagerly waiting for her yearly visits. I tell him I will make sure that I tell her that.

Socorro surprised me with a beautiful small straw doll she made for me. This is so you won't forget us, she said as she handed it to me. I will never forget you, I assure her. And I promised to be back soon. At this time Fernando and Laura finally join us at the table for breakfast.

When I finish breakfast, I excuse myself and go to the main house to get my luggage. I take one last look at the little corner where I comfortably slept for a few months. I will never forget this little corner that was made just for me. Now that I understand all that goes on here, this is a wonderful place. The little table with the can flower vase. Tia Maria embroiders the pillows. The warm blanket knitted by Rafaela and so on. What a unique and wonderful little corner this is. It will always live in my heart. I step out of the curtains to take one last look at the family pictures on the wall. So many memories and life stories on this wall. Generations lived life here as best as they could. They all made a future for future generations.

I have come to understand and accept things that happen. One thing brings another and only God knows why or how? I have come to learn and accept that things aren't always right, that pain at times is deep and overwhelming, and that time heals everything. I thank God for my awakening. I now know that life and death are all the same. *"You can be living a dead life, or you can decide to live again."* **"You can live your life in peace, or live your life in pieces."**

Saying goodbye here is in a sense, so warm and beautiful. I feel the love coming to me to be real and sincere. They ask me when I'm coming back to visit. I tell them as soon as possible, but I'll come with Eddie and Jose next time. They like that.

Fernando and Laura are also now finished with their breakfast and are ready to start the trip back to the city. I say my final goodbye to the women and thank everyone for their hospitality. I can see one or two tears in their eyes. Tia Maria comes to me to bless me and calls me her new "daughter," and by now, I'm overwhelmed with emotion.

I finally get in the car, it's time to go, Fernando says, and we begin to drive off. As I turn back, I can still see the whole group standing in the middle of the street waving goodbye. Tia Maria blesses us from afar again. I feel like a brand new person now. I will miss the people and the places here in La Laja. But I can't wait to get home to my family in Los Angeles.

Chapter 65
Back Home In Los Angeles

I have been home for a while now, and am so happy to be with my family. Things here are good and not so different. Things have not changed at all, but what's changed is my perspective in life and the way I see things now, which makes the difference. Everyone tells me that I look rested and that I seem like a different person, especially my husband. He says I look like I found peace. I don't have to explain much to him because he knows exactly what I went through and why he sent me there. Eddie seems to be the happiest with my return home. We will be taking Mommy and me classes soon. There is still lots of work to do with him, and we are all a family. At this time I feel I am the happiest and luckiest woman on earth.

Returning to the city after months in the countryside is an eye-opening experience for me. First of all, I have come to appreciate the privileges offered in the city. I'd like to begin with, of course, number one is having a bathroom inside the house, with no little creatures in it to be afraid of. I never before thought about this being such a great convenient necessity and, most of all, a privilege. Flushing a toilet for the first time in months was music to my ears.

Having doctors, hospitals, and clinics nearby is comforting to know in case of any sudden illness or emergency. Not having the added burden of having to drive hours to the nearest medical help is very comforting. I never thought of this before. During my son's illness, finding a hospital was the least of my worries, and I'm now so grateful for that.

Having a variety of foods, fruits, and vegetables available at our fingertips at any time of the year is a real blessing. It's something we all take for granted. We have no concept of weather or season connecting to our food. Most of us have no idea where our meals come from, or what some people have to do hard work for us to have food on our table.

Having modern city luxuries like washers and dryers instead of washing in the river again took me to another perspective in time and even to the present time in places like La Laja. Televisions, cars, and transportation methods are a true modern blessing. And what can I say about the "telephone" The telephone is a lifeline when a loved one is so far away.

These are all things I took for granted living here in Los Angeles. I now notice people's relationships get easily lost in a big city such as this. I must confess that I don't even know my neighbor, even though we've lived here for more than five years, I don't know who lives in the house next to me. Life here seems more impersonal and more individualistic.

I still miss my son Xavier, but now it's clear to me that all that has happened was and is meant to be. I still visit his tomb, but now only once a week. I know he's not in his tomb but in heaven and my heart. A few months ago before my trip, I never thought I would ever be able to stop coming to the cemetery even one day. I can see how crazy and out of control I was thinking that Xavier was here and that I had to be here to take care of him.

Living in Los Angeles, I quickly re-adjusted myself to my daily life routine and family. Visiting family and friends, having barbecues with the family, going shopping, and to the movies with my sisters all came back to me easily. I'm so happy that my old self is almost fully restored. My friends and family are also pleased with my return. They let me know how comforting it is for them to see me like this. My family is unsure of what happened to me in Mexico or what I went through in the village, but "whatever it is" they say," they are very pleased with the results." I can see the happiness they feel for me reflected in their eyes. I try to tell them that life never stopped, it just took me in a whole new direction.

Almost a year after visiting La Laja, Jose and I decide to take a quick two-week vacation together there. This time we decided to bring Eddie along. We are so happy that Eddie too is going to Mexico with us. We are looking forward to seeing the whole family in La Laja, and I am so excited to see the women and everyone else again. Jose can't wait to see his family after being gone for seven long years. Like the one before, this trip promises to be unique and rewarding for all involved.

CHAPTER 66
GOING TO TOYS R US

JUNE 13, 1983

Today I promised Eddie that we would go to Toys R US after breakfast and buy him a new toy. He is very excited to do this, but mostly I believe he and I are just happy to finally spend lots of time together. In the last weeks back home we have been visiting the park and the library every day, and just spending time together as mother and son. At night before bedtime, he loves me to read him stories about dinosaurs and superheroes, especially the "HeMan" and "Superman" stories.

Arriving at Toys R Us and in the store's parking lot, Eddie reminds me that he wants to buy a Superman with a red cape. I smile at him and tell him of course. He smiles back and I hold his little hand and walk across the parking lot and into the store. His request made me think about the children of La Laja who have no real toys to play with but are happy making their own. I think how lucky Eddie is to be able to choose and get a toy that he wants. He has no idea how lucky he is, and how lucky I am as a parent to be able to buy it for him.

After so many months of not being in a city, walking into this store like this is overwhelming for me. There are toys everywhere in Toys R Us. There are bicycles, trucks, kitchen sets, and dolls of all kinds. Colorful plastic balls, telephones, and horses. Walking through the aisles with Eddie sitting in the shopping cart I see some toys that I had not noticed before. New Super Heroes. Eddie and I take this section slowly, looking at one doll at a time, until we finally spot Superman with the red cape that he wants. Eddie is now happy with his toy in hand and then says he wants to go home and play with it.

Walking towards the cashier, I come across the doll section. At first, I walk directly through the long section without paying much attention to it, but then I come across the baby dolls section and a sign that says: *"two for one sale."* I see newborn dolls, lots of beautiful baby dolls with beautiful dresses and different colored hair. My heart skips a beat thinking about what these dolls will mean for the women back in La Laja. I remember how much they, as small children, wished to have a "real" doll of their own. Every doll I look at reminds me of each woman. My heart is speaking to me right now.

By now Eddie notices my distraction and is trying to get my attention " Mommy, mommy! "I want to go home and play with my Superman." Hearing this brings me back to Eddie. For seconds my mind escaped to La Laja. We will go home soon son. Just let me just pick up some dolls. The first doll I picked up is a beautiful blond doll with a blue dress, just like the one Tia Maria described in her memory. Eddie looks at the doll and asks me "Is that your doll?" Mommy. I tell him it was for my friend.

Continuing in my walk through the doll aisle, I see two other dolls that I believe to be perfect, one boy doll for Rafaela, who lost a young son, and a baby doll for Regina who loves babies. Now I stop at a set of twin dolls, a boy and a girl dressed in matching clothes. I decide these dolls would be good for Marina for the two children she lost in the river. I was so amazed to find the Barbie section, where I found a Barbie doll sewing with a sewing machine, and so I chose this doll for Socorro. Then I see a Barbie, a"teacher Barbie" with a chalkboard and so this one would be for Elena. Then I remembered Dona Christina. I looked around for the perfect doll for her. I found a beautiful chubby cheek doll that I think she would love to hold. By this time, Eddie is asking me why I put so many dolls in the basket. They're for my friends in Mexico, I tell him. "Your friends are little girls," he asks. Yes, they are little girls, I answer him with a smile on my face.

When Eddie and I get home from shopping, Jose notices the bags of dolls I drop off on the sofa. "What are these bags of dolls about," he asks quickly. "Who's dolls are these?" "They are dolls for La Laja." I answered him. "But there are more than eight little girls living in La Laja," he says. "No, these dolls are not for the children of La Laja. They are for the eight women in the compound." "What?" "These dolls are for women of the compound in La Laja? I don't understand, why women? What are you talking about?" I think that for a minute there Jose thinks I'm going "wacko."

I begin to explain that the last thing I did in La Laja was to do a little childhood regression exercise with the women of the compound. "The women were excited and very curious to know what this exercise was all about?". "They made arrangements to have enough time to do the whole exercise, and when the day came they were all ready to do the exercise, which was about their childhood toys."

"What I soon came to find out in this exercise was that they all never really have toys or even time to play and most importantly that they all forever wish was to someday have a doll of their own." "I see where you're going," Jose said right away.

"Throughout the exercise, the women all shared their different childhood scenarios with me, and one of the things that they all had in common was the fact, like I told you, that as children they always wanted to have a real doll and not a straw one like most of them did".

"Today without any planning, as I was shopping for Eddie's superhero, I came across the doll aisle and saw these dolls on sale, and I suddenly got the idea in my heart of buying these dolls for them." I tell Jose. " I can tell that the families and people there really touched you. You have a good heart," he tells me, "you are giving them so much by giving them these dolls." "And they have given so much too," I tell him. "I can't wait to see the women's faces when I surprise them with the dolls." "I want to see that too," he says with enthusiasm.

I held on to the dolls until it was time to return to La Laja.

CHAPTER 67
RE-VISITING LA LAJA

Everyone in Laja is surprised and happy to see the whole family come to visit. Tio Juan IS especially happy to see his sister's child Jose, return home after so long. We arrived in the evening, and as before, we were greeted with lots of warmth and love. Fernando and Laura drove us here and the family is happy to see them too.

The Patio is again gleaming with decorations of flowers and pretty colored embroidered tablecloths. The women made Jose's favorite dishes and Tio Juan and Tia Maria can't stop crying because they are so happy to finally see Jose returning home, after seven long years. The three cried when they remembered the day he and his family first left the village to look for a better life. Tio Juan thanks Jose for trusting them by sending his wife back to his home to heal.

The feast continues with everyone at the large table, including the children, who by now have already made friends and are playing with Eddie. The conversations around the table are filled with memories and funny stories about how Jose lived his childhood here and his adventures as a mischievous little boy. Tio Juan talks about the sad morning when his sister, her husband, and children left La Laja on a small donkey with very little food to travel a long distance across the mountains. His eyes teared up when he said how much he worried about them making it to the city.

Jose adds a conversation about the long days he and his family spent crossing the high Sierra surviving mostly on water, cacti, and some roots. " It was a hard and terrifying journey," he says. "As a child, I remember my father and mother crying and praying to find refuge from the rain and heat that at times lured them to the mountainsides." "When we finally got close to the city light one night, we rejoiced."

Tio Juan and Tia Maria agreed that their move was risky but all for the best. Soon the conversation switched over to a lighter tone. Now the conversation is about my first visit to La Laja. Regina said how lost and awkward I seemed to be when I first arrived here, especially around the kitchen and the outhouse. Everyone laughs, including me.

Retelling my adventures in the outhouse is especially funny to them still. Rafaela says she admires how little by little I became more and more comfortable with everything here, and how fast they got to know me and really like me. I feel good to hear that and to be back to visit. I feel their genuine warmth in a very welcoming conversation is loving to all of us. This visit is very different now because I am returning as a family member.

The conversation then goes to Jose's childhood adventures. He used to dare to take his grandfather's only horse from the stable without permission and ride it all day in the Sierra, while everyone worried about him and the horse. There were wild animals to look out for and Jose was just a child but a brave child. But the story that the whole town knows to this date is about when Jose was playing with a little cat in the family's small kitchen. Jose's mother left a large boiling pot on the wood stove and told her children to stay away from it. Jose went into the kitchen chasing a small cat. He got a hold of it and began tossing the cat up to the straw roof and wooden beams, where the cat's claws would catch and hold on for a bit and fall again. Jose found this amusing. He would catch the cat repeatedly until he threw the cat too close to the boiling pot and the cat fell short of reaching the ceiling and straight into the boiling pot of atole.

The cat quickly jumped out of the boiling pot screeching and ran out of the kitchen and into a small cornfield. Everyone that was there could see the trail of white and gray smoke the cat was leaving behind him. Jose was feeling bad because he knew that the *atole* in the pot was the only meal the whole family would have that night. Ashamed and afraid of seeing his mother, he took off to the mountain. When it got dark his mother worried about him and hoped he would return soon.

Soon Jose returned home with his head done and waiting to be scolded, and before his mother said anything he began to quietly giggle. What are you giggling about? His mother asked. "I remember the trail of smoke the cat was leaving behind as he ran through the fields and into the small creek. It looked really funny" he said. Everyone at the table laughed at the story as they all have before, for they know the story very well. Even small children know the story too. Jose's story is famous here in La Laja Tio Antonio said laughing and holding his belly.

In the middle of all the laughing and eating, Elena and her husband suddenly walk into the patio and surprise everyone. Elena happily greets everyone, turns to me, and gives me a warm and strong embrace. "It's so good to see you again, and I'm especially happy Jose and Eddie are here with you." Elena is gleaming with happiness. I can tell not only that she is in love with her husband, but very content in her career as a teacher.

Elena then introduces her husband to us. She explains to us that they are just returning from Guadalajara from a state teacher conference. They happily share the news that they will be getting a little school soon to service the children of the area. "Many changes are being done here in La Laja and surrounding villages in terms of education," Jose Luis explains very excitingly.

I am so happy to see Elena and Jose like this. Their excitement is so contagious to everyone here. Elena shares with me how she's been teaching the children the dances I taught her, and wants me to teach her some more dances. She says the children enjoy dancing, Especially Dona Tomasa's grandchildren. I was happy to hear this. I was especially happy to hear that Dona Tomasa's grandchildren were in school. It is clear to me that Elena is enjoying her new life and all her blessings.

Rafaela and Marina take me aside to tell me how happy they are to see me again. That I look good and very peaceful and content. I tell them that I owe all this to all of them. They then tell me how my visit here also greatly impacted their lives. This made me feel really good inside.

Rafaela is the first to ask me if I could play the game of regression again before I leave for Los Angeles again. I told her, "I already have one planned session for them, a very special one." Upon hearing these words, the women get so excited that the men wonder why there's such a commotion with the women around them in the kitchen.

After dinner, the women begin to clean up the kitchen table and dishes, and the men decide to do as always, sit on the patio and talk about their harvest with Jose and Fernando. They believe they will have a good harvest this year, they say to Jose as he joins them. " How is the family in Los Angeles Jose?" Tio Juan asks. "I wish they would come to visit more often or soon before I die," he says.

The conversations return to when Jose was a young boy and how he used to help the men in the harvests. Don Juan says Jose was a good and responsible boy, always willing to help in the fields. "My sister raised you right," Tio Antonio says as he pats Jose's back with great love and respect. Jose returns the gesture with a sincere hug and both men continue the conversation with the group.

As the evening falls and night comes in, it's now time to go to sleep. Fernando and Laura decide to spend the night and leave for the city the next morning. Regina invites them to stay in their house for the night. Rafaela leads us to her house, but this time we are taken to her and Manuel's bed and bedroom, where they have already made accommodations with a small bed for Eddie to sleep next to us. Manuel and Rafaela make sure we have a comfortable place to stay.

Eddie has already fallen asleep in my arms. He has had a long day with the trip and playing with the children. I clean him up as much as I can, put on his pajamas, and put him down in the soft bed next to our bed. Both Jose and I need to visit the outhouse. It was not as scary for me this time because Jose's company made me feel safe. This time it's not as frightening as it was the first time. With Jose I didn't fear finding any little creatures, he was there to take care of me. My hero!

Lying in bed with Jose and my son next to me is a dream come true. I had this dream many nights as I lay in my bed alone. Jose tells me, " I feel so lucky to have come back here to visit my family." Looking out at the moon through the side window reminds mJosehe many nights this very moon was my only company. I also come to think of Xavier at this time. I know that he is very happy I found myself and that we are here altogether. Now, no matter where I am, or where I go he is with me. I thank God for this day, this family, and this life. I believe I'm blessed in every way. Lying here with my husband and my son in La Laja makes me feel complete. Jose was right, I did find my peace here.

I feel now it's a good time to let Jose know that we will be parents again. That I am three months pregnant and that I wanted to surprise him with the news here in La Laja. Jose is overwhelmed with happiness and holds me even tighter to say I love you. "God will bless us again with a healthy child, I'm sure of that," he says with total confidence." "What great news! Eddie is going to have a little playmate." "God is good," I tell Jose. "Yes, he is," I tell him. Amen!

August 27, 1983

It's a new morning and Jose has gotten up early to milk the cows with his cousins. He has taken Eddie with him for the experience. As I'm getting up Rafaela comes into the room to inform me that she has heated some water for my morning bath. I can tell she's very happy for me to have my little family here.

After my bath, I go to the kitchen where most of the men and Jose are already enjoying a hearty breakfast, complete with handmade tortillas. I see Eddie sitting in the Patio with the kids playing with some wooden and clay toys. "Buenos Dias," the women all greet me with a smile. "We have made your favorite for breakfast." The women serve my favorite, "chilaquiles" with beans and cheese. After breakfast, Fernando and Laura are also enjoying their breakfast and soon announce their departure back to the city. They thank everyone for the great meal. We accompany them to their car and say goodbye. See you soon they tell Jose as they give us one last hug. We watch them drive down the hillside and fade into the main road. Now it's time to go and continue our day.

By now Regina gets close to me to inform me that Jose has agreed to keep the men busy on the fields so that we can have our game today. He has also agreed to take Eddie with him to show him the horses up in the mountain. Everyone will be out of the compound for a few hours. We are free to have a session with you. The women seem to be very anxious to play again. It seems they have made all the accommodations. We finished preparing the mid-day meal to be free again all morning. The children are in school and the older children will be doing their chores. Everything is set, Regina eagerly said. Even Marina seemed excited about our meeting.

Both Socorro and Rafaela arrange to use the large room as before. All the chairs are set in a circle. Dona Maria brought her sister Christina again with her. By the middle of the morning, the group is now complete and ready to start. Without me saying a word this time, the women are all sitting and set, ready to start. I close the curtains and tell them to close their eyes and try to concentrate. Once again, I ask them to take deep breaths in through the nose and out through their mouth. The ladies seem to have been practicing because their breathing is easier this time.

I ask them to visualize a place with beautiful flowers of different colors. The Mountainside in full bloom. As the women are visualizing, I pull the suitcase filled with dolls quietly into the center of the circle. I ask them to visualize a waterfall right next to them and to feel its breeze. Now, I tell them that " it's time to go back to their childhood and to think about how they wished to one day have a doll." I ask them "How do you think about how they would feel to finally have one?" I then ask them "to keep their eyes closed and put their arms out in front of them. I tell them that no matter what they felt in their hands, they were to keep their arms out and not to open their eyes for any reason until I told them to do so."

The women nod in agreement. I quietly opened the suitcase and pull out the first doll. It is a blonde doll with a blue dress. I place her in Tia Maria's arms. And remind her to keep her eyes closed. Then I pick up the twin dolls and placed them in Marina's trembling arms. Next, I pick up the Barbie doll with the sewing machine for Socorro. Then I give Rafaela her chunky baby boy. I hand Regina the doll she always wanted, with beautiful long brown hair.

The last baby/doll I deliver is the chunky baby doll to Chistina. The night before I managed to pull the doll's right hand out, to be just like Christina. When my deliveries were done and over, I slowly opened the curtains and told them to slowly open their eyes and see what they were holding in their arms.

When the women first open their eyes they seem a bit confused about what was going on in front of them. The room now is fully lit and bright. Little by little they began to realize what they were holding and quickly ask: " What's this, are these dolls for us?" t "Yes they are your dolls," I tell them, and soon the tears of joy begin to fall. The happiness felt in the room could be sustained or held back. It was overwhelming.

Tia Maria said that her doll was exactly like the doll the farm owner's daughter was playing with the day she saw her in the big Hacienda house! "How did you find her?" Tia Maria asks me in the middle of her tears. "She is exactly like the one I saw in the farmhouse." I walk over to Marina to find her in a state of disbelief at what she was holding in her arms. "My babies!'' she cries as she presses the dolls hard in her chest. "These are my babies!" She says again and again, with tears of joy! "They are back in my arms."

Regina and Socorro gleam with happiness in looking at their Barbies. 'I can't believe it! a little sewing machine for me" Regina says. 'My doll is beautiful, just like in my dreams'! Socorro adds. Elena was so happy to finally get her teacher Barbie doll! With a little plastic chalkboard and desk. "Gracias muchas gracias!" Elena says. I always dreamed of playing with this."

And now it is time to see Christina and her doll. Christina is profoundly touched to see that her doll is missing her right hand just like her. She breaks down with emotion and happy tears. "She's just like me!" She says loudly, speaking out for the first time since the incident. Everyone is astonished to hear her finally speak.

Cristina then takes her hand out of her apron pocket in front of all the women for the very first time in many years and holds her beautiful doll up in the air. "My doll is just like me!" She screams again with her hand and doll up in the air. Soon the women see Doña Christina in tears and they also begin to cry happy tears for her. Everyone, including me, is moved by this special moment.

Soon the rest of the women continue playing with their dolls. "Thank you, gracias for my baby boy," Rafaela says. "I needed this" "Muchas gracias for giving me a little part of my child again," Marina tells me as she hugs me. "I feel I'm holding them again, a part of my children is back with me again."

I now announce to them that they all have some special time to play with their dolls before it's time to go back to their chores. Without hesitation, the women begin to play, sing, cuddle, and share their dolls among themselves. Rafaela softly cradles her son and sings beautiful lullabies. Marina holds her dolls/children tight and tells them "She misses them and loves them." Regina pretends to be sewing in her little sewing machine and dressing her Barbie. Tia Maria keeps staring at her doll's dress and plays with the blue ribbon on her hair. Elena begins to teach with her little desk and chalkboard. Christina cradles her doll and kisses the little arm with the missing hand. And Socorro combs her dolls and long hair, trying to braid it.

This is so tender and beautiful for my eyes and heart to keep. I'm exploding with joy. It is true that *"it is better to give than to receive."* These moments are now imprinted in my soul forever. I will always remember this day to be the day of the *"Muñecas"* The day these women became little girls to recover and heal their childhood for a few minutes. And to some become real and complete mothers in recovering the symbols of their dead children. I am fortunate to see these women in their full happiness. It's as though a full circle has come to a close. A spiritual awakening occurred in all of us in that room.

My Conclusion

"**Muñecas**" are not only dolls, but they could be an overwhelming, intense, magical, and peaceful feeling inside your soul, given to you in time of need. It could be praying, meditating, writing, jogging, dancing, etc. Everyone is different in their search. Holding these "dolls," or doing what comforts your being, gives a sense of understanding, and you will eventually have a re-encounter within. The feeling of trespassing death and holding on to the hope of one day being together once more then becomes real. Whether the loss is a child or adult, is all the same when encountering this inner peace. A **Muñeca** can symbolize a friend, a place, a hobby, spiritual comfort, a journey, or anything that speaks to your soul and allows you to spread your wings. And with open arms, comfort you in your time of need.

Now a new veil of understanding is revealed to me through this journey. I'm so grateful for this. Now I know my son chose me as his mother to teach me a great lesson of love and belief. This made me the woman I am today. He taught me that LOVE runs in all of us and if we allow it, it will fill our lives with greater peace. *Mi Camino,* or my Journey to La Laja was a significant turning point in my life. A sort of inner spiritual awakening. I call this very special moment with these women "The Journey of*: "Muñecas."* And the beauty is the unity, compassion, and sharing we had with one another. We became **one.** Each of these women is in fact a beautiful Muñeca, inside and out. We all are.

"The sand is great in numbers, but each grain is exactly the same." This is what I was searching for, to feel the same.

The *toughest part of life is "death." But there, I now know there is hope.*

Muñecas

October 18, 2021

Jose's journey on earth with me ended October 18, 2021. He left quickly and simply as he was. Sadness invades my heart, but this time I know how to handle and understand the death process and its purpose.

One of my teachers in life was Jose. He enjoyed his life to the fullest and lived as he wanted, free and enjoying everyday life as it came. He knew how to live. Our marriage, like so many other marriages, was not perfect. At times it was very difficult to live and to understand each other, and at times it was a joyful road to travel together. Like every marriage, we lived a real roller coaster of ups and downs and survived 43 years together. We both knew that deep underneath it all, we loved each other.

Now he is with beloved ancestors, in a place where they keep an eye on us. Now he is with his son Xavier and waits for me to join them one day.

People that cross our paths in life and intertwine with our souls teach us many lessons. Jose's journey with me was to carry me through my heavy journey of losing my son. He walked with me every step of the way. He taught me that the most hurtful experiences leave the best lessons of love and humility.

I have come to understand that these lessons are meant to allow us to become better and complete human beings with real merit. Best of all, our journey allows us to in the end become the person we are meant to be.

Losing someone you love is very difficult and painful. For most of us, death is hard to understand. Through my losses, I have learned that mourning is a different process for each person and for each time it happens. This process has many levels. But when walking deep throughout every level, one can begin to see and understand the purpose of that person's life being in your life. Most importantly, it brings the understanding that our lives are a gift to one another. *Thank You, Jose, for the journey we shared together. "Por el camino compartido."*

"Te amaré Siempre."

In Loving Memory of Jose Lopez Becerra "Chema"

October 21, 1955 - October 18, 2021

Our Journey

1979

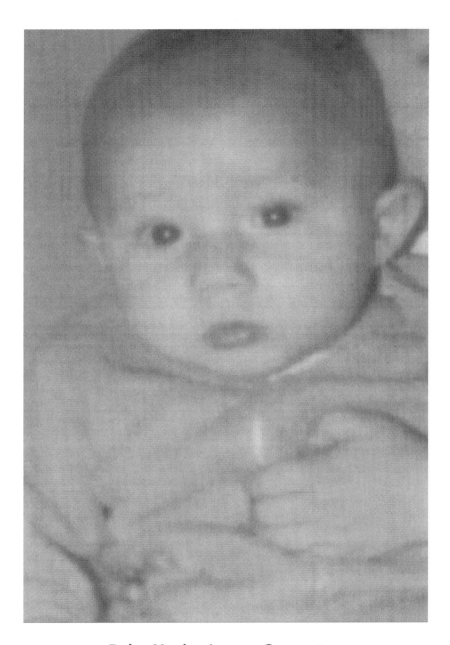

Baby Xavier Lopez Cervantes

GLOSSARY

Abuelita	Grandmother
Abuelito	Grandfather
Angelitos	Angels
Antojitos	Various Mexican dishes
Ayudenme	Help me
Bano de Jicara	Bathing with a bucket
Bastardo	Fatherless son/daughter
Buenos dias	Good Morning
Canela	Cinnamon
Comadre	Best friend/ child's godmother
Cuarentena	Best friend/ child's godmother
Curandera	Medicine woman
Dia de Muertos	Day of the Dead
Doña	Elderly woman
El Grito	Mexican Holiday (16 0f September)
Frijoles	Beans
Guadaluoe	Virgen Mary

Istafiate	Herb
Jarro	Mexican mug
La Laja	Village
Lavador	Place to wash clothes
Lo que Dios Mande	What God decides
Miguel Hidalgo	A Mexican Hero of independence
Mija/Mijo	A term of endearment
Munecas	Dolls
Niño,Niña	Young girl and boy
Noche Buena	Christmas Eve
Pan dulce	Mexican sweat bread
Papel picaddo	Colorful decoration paper
Pasillo	Hallway
Pila	Tub
Que pasa	What is going on
Rancho	Ranch
Ruda	Wild herb
Senora	Respectful name for Mrs.
Servilletas	Napkins
Soppes	Round small tortilla with meat and cheese
Tienda	Store

Tortear	The act of making tortillas
Yerbabuena	Peppermint
Yerbera	Herbal healer